Holy Manipulation

Freedom from Spiritual Abuse and Religious Narcissism –
Techniques to Reclaim Your Voice, Break the Cycle, and
Find Peace Beyond the Pulpit

Nicci Brochard
&
Dr. Ben Chuba

Holy Manipulation

Freedom from Spiritual Abuse and Religious Narcissism –
Techniques to Reclaim Your Voice, Break the Cycle, and
Find Peace Beyond the Pulpit

Book Formatting by: Monisha

Book cover design by: *Billy Design*

CROSSBORDER

New York, London, Quebec

Contents

Chapter 12: Becoming the Voice You Needed – Advocacy, Art, and Impact.. 99

Chapter 13: Holy Liberation – Peace That No Preacher Can Take Away..108

Epilogue...118

Introduction

In faith and religious world, the sanctuary is meant to be a place of refuge, healing, and spiritual growth. Yet for many, it becomes a space of manipulation, control, and emotional trauma. "Holy Manipulation: Freedom from Spiritual Abuse and Religious Narcissism" explores the painful reality of spiritual abuse and the toxic dynamics that can occur in religious communities. It takes an honest and unflinching look at how narcissistic leaders and manipulative practices can create environments where individuals feel trapped, invalidated, and disempowered. For those who have endured this kind of spiritual abuse, this book offers a guide to reclaiming their voice, breaking free from the cycle, and finding true peace beyond the pulpit.

Spiritual abuse can be subtle but profound, often disguised as a form of caring or divine intervention. Charismatic leaders use religious texts and beliefs to assert control, distort power, and manipulate followers into submission. Whether through guilt, fear, isolation, or emotional coercion, these leaders exploit their authority for personal gain, while leaving their congregants emotionally scarred. The abuse isn't always physical or obvious; it's a slow erosion of one's self-worth, a manipulation of faith, and a systematic silencing of personal autonomy.

At its core, spiritual abuse thrives on the vulnerability of individuals seeking a deeper connection with God. Religious narcissism is a dangerous and destructive element that can go unnoticed until it has already taken a hold of the victim's life. Narcissistic leaders often disguise their behavior with an aura of piety, convincing followers that their actions are God-ordained or spiritually righteous. This form of manipulation feeds on the sacred trust people place in spiritual figures, creating a power imbalance that benefits the leader at the expense of the believer's well-being.

In the face of this abuse, it is not uncommon for individuals to lose their sense of self, their trust in others, and sometimes even their faith in God. Many victims struggle with the shame and guilt of feeling like they have somehow failed or fallen short of the divine expectations imposed on them by their abuser. However, the truth is that spiritual abuse is not a reflection of their faith or their worth; it is a direct result of the corruptive misuse of power within the religious community.

"Holy Manipulation" provides not only an understanding of the psychological and spiritual damage caused by these toxic relationships but also offers practical techniques for breaking free from the cycle of abuse. It explores how individuals can regain control of their spiritual journey and start the process of healing. This journey of recovery involves confronting painful truths, rediscovering one's personal relationship with God, and rebuilding trust in a way that empowers rather than diminishes.

The book encourages readers to embrace their autonomy, reclaim their voice, and find peace beyond the pulpit. It introduces powerful strategies to confront and dismantle the manipulative tactics used by narcissistic leaders, offering a pathway to freedom that allows for spiritual authenticity. It's a call to reclaim the narrative of one's spiritual journey— not dictated by the voices of others but guided by one's own heart, soul, and understanding of divine love.

By sharing personal stories, insights from experts, and actionable steps for recovery, "Holy Manipulation" provides a roadmap for those who have felt silenced or diminished in their spiritual lives. It is a beacon of hope for those who wish to break free from religious narcissism, heal from the trauma of spiritual abuse, and create a renewed, empowered relationship with their faith that is rooted in freedom, peace, and authenticity.

This book is more than just a guide; it is a movement toward spiritual liberation. It serves as a powerful reminder that faith should be a source of empowerment, not oppression, and that reclaiming your voice is the first step toward healing and peace.

Ben and I (Nicci) thank you immensely for choosing this book. You promise you will find in t what you are looking for. Thank you.

PART I
UNHOLY GROUND – UNDERSTANDING SPIRITUAL ABUSE

Chapter 1

The Wolf in the Robe – What Is Spiritual Abuse?

Spiritual abuse is a term that, for many, invokes a range of emotions: confusion, anger, shame, and, at times, disbelief. After all, how could someone who claims to represent God or a higher spiritual authority use that very power to exploit and manipulate others? Unfortunately, this abuse is far more prevalent than most people realize, and it transcends traditional religious institutions, cult-like environments, and even mainstream religious settings. This chapter delves into the concept of spiritual abuse, how it manifests, and the various ways in which power dynamics are twisted in the name of faith.

Defining Spiritual Abuse in Religious, Cult-like, and Mainstream Settings

Spiritual abuse can be defined as the exploitation of a person's spiritual beliefs or practices by someone in a position of power. This type of abuse is unique in that it specifically targets an individual's most intimate, deeply held beliefs and uses those beliefs against them for the abuser's personal gain. While spiritual abuse is often associated with organized religion or cults, it can also occur in more mainstream religious settings or even in informal spiritual groups. The context doesn't necessarily matter as much as the abusive dynamics of control, manipulation, and psychological harm.

In religious or cult-like settings, spiritual abuse is most often perpetrated by leaders who position themselves as divinely appointed or spiritually superior figures. These individuals often claim a unique connection to God, higher powers, or spiritual insight, thus gaining access to the deepest aspects of their followers' lives. In these environments, spiritual abuse might manifest as guilt-tripping, demanding sacrifices of time or resources, and manipulating followers into submitting to their will. Cult leaders, for example, may use their claimed divine authority to demand complete obedience, often alienating individuals from their families, friends, and wider communities.

However, spiritual abuse isn't confined to extreme or fringe religious settings. It also occurs within more mainstream religious environments, sometimes in subtler forms. In these cases, spiritual leaders may abuse their position of authority by exploiting their followers' trust, manipulating scripture, or taking advantage of personal vulnerabilities. Mainstream religious settings are not immune to the presence of narcissistic leaders who exploit the sacred to serve their own ego-driven agendas. Unfortunately, those within these settings may not recognize the signs of spiritual abuse because they are accustomed to the authority figures being trusted without question. In these contexts, spiritual abuse often takes the form of emotional manipulation, coercion, and even isolation from others in the name of faith.

One of the defining aspects of spiritual abuse, regardless of the setting, is the abuser's ability to exploit the inherent trust placed in them by their followers. Spiritual leaders often capitalize on the belief that their guidance is divinely inspired, which makes it difficult for followers to question their authority or recognize the abuse. Spiritual abuse can occur subtly over time, with a leader slowly eroding an individual's sense of self, faith, and autonomy under the guise of helping them grow spiritually.

Power Dynamics in the Name of God

At the core of spiritual abuse lies a disturbing distortion of power. Spiritual leaders are often placed on a pedestal, seen as mediators between God and their followers. This creates a highly unequal power dynamic. Followers, believing that their spiritual leader has a unique connection to the divine, relinquish their personal power and autonomy, placing their trust in someone they believe will lead them to salvation, enlightenment, or spiritual fulfillment. In an ideal spiritual community, this power dynamic would be one of mutual respect, guidance, and support. But in cases of spiritual abuse, the power imbalance becomes a weapon.

When a spiritual leader uses their position to dominate, control, or manipulate others, they distort the very concept of spiritual authority. The leader becomes not a guide, but a gatekeeper who controls access to divine truth, spiritual growth, or even salvation itself. They often claim to have a direct line to God, making their words or actions infallible in the eyes of their followers. This manipulation of spiritual authority is particularly insidious because it taps into the deepest fears and desires of individuals: the fear of being disconnected from God, the desire for divine approval, and the need to belong to a community that offers safety and guidance.

In such an environment, questioning the leader's authority may feel like questioning God. This is a potent tool for maintaining control over followers. The leader may even accuse individuals of being spiritually immature, lacking faith, or being sinful if they resist or question the established norms. This type of manipulation exploits the follower's trust, and fear is often instilled through the threat of eternal consequences, such as spiritual punishment or damnation. By framing spiritual questioning as rebellion or sin, the abuser effectively isolates the individual from any external sources of support, making it all the more difficult to break free from the cycle of abuse.

The power dynamics at play in spiritual abuse are also reinforced by social pressure. Many religious communities emphasize communal unity and togetherness, and the fear of exclusion from that community can be overwhelming. A leader might isolate individuals from their families or peers, or demand that they prioritize their relationship with the religious group above all else. This isolation ensures that the follower has no outside perspective or support to challenge the manipulation and control they are experiencing.

It's important to note that power dynamics are not always as overt as demanding submission or isolation. More often, they manifest as a constant, subtle erosion of the individual's sense of self-worth. A leader might employ techniques such as gaslighting, where the follower is made to doubt their perceptions and experiences, or they may use "spiritual" justifications to demand excessive sacrifices. These tactics wear down the individual's mental, emotional, and spiritual resilience, making it increasingly difficult for them to recognize or challenge the abuse.

Emotional, Psychological, and Social Manipulation

Spiritual abuse is often insidious because it works on multiple levels: emotionally, psychologically, and socially. On an emotional level, spiritual abusers manipulate their followers by preying on their vulnerabilities. Many individuals turn to religion or spirituality in times of hardship, confusion, or crisis, and abusers exploit these moments of emotional fragility. The manipulator may present themselves as a source of comfort and guidance, offering solace in exchange for complete devotion and submission. This emotional dependence is a powerful tool in the abuser's arsenal, as it makes the follower feel incapable of navigating their spiritual journey without the leader's direction.

The emotional manipulation doesn't stop with just offering guidance; it often includes guilt-tripping, shaming, or playing on fears. For instance, the abuser may tell the follower that their struggles are a result of their lack of faith or sinfulness, or that they will never be "truly blessed" unless they comply with the abuser's demands. This emotional manipulation leaves the follower feeling confused, ashamed, and afraid to trust their own instincts or beliefs. It also instills a constant sense of inadequacy, which makes the follower more susceptible to further control.

Psychologically, spiritual abuse often leads to long-term trauma, as the follower internalizes the manipulative messages of the abuser. Over time, the individual may come to believe that they are unworthy of love or spiritual fulfillment unless they adhere to the abuser's teachings or demands. This self-blame and self-doubt can become deeply ingrained, making it difficult for the individual to recognize the abuse as it unfolds. The manipulation of personal identity and autonomy is a powerful aspect of spiritual abuse, and it often leads to a profound sense of confusion, disorientation, and emotional numbness.

On a social level, spiritual abuse operates by isolating the victim from other perspectives or sources of support. In extreme cases, the abuser may demand that followers cut ties with family and friends who do not share the same religious views or who question the leader's authority. This social isolation is designed to create an environment where the follower has nowhere else to turn but to the abuser. Even in less extreme cases, spiritual abusers may subtly or overtly create divisions within a community, fostering an "us vs. them" mentality that further alienates individuals from the outside world.

The social manipulation also extends to the way in which the community reinforces the abuser's authority. Social norms and expectations within the religious group may be tailored to ensure that everyone adheres to the leader's teachings, with those who deviate from the norm being marginalized or ostracized. The fear of social exclusion within the community is another potent tool used by abusers to maintain control.

In summary, spiritual abuse is a multifaceted phenomenon that draws on power dynamics, emotional and psychological manipulation, and social isolation. It is a form of exploitation that targets the most intimate aspects of an individual's identity— their faith, their beliefs, and their connection to the divine. Whether it occurs in a cult-like environment or within a more mainstream religious setting, spiritual abuse is a harmful and often devastating experience. The journey to healing and reclaiming one's voice involves recognizing these dynamics, breaking free from the grip of manipulation, and rediscovering one's authentic spiritual path. This chapter has only scratched the surface of what spiritual abuse looks like and how it operates, but it serves as a foundational understanding for the healing process that will be explored in the following chapters.

Conclusion:

Spiritual abuse is a pernicious and often hidden form of manipulation that exploits the deepest aspects of an individual's life— their faith, their beliefs, and their sense of self. Whether occurring in a religious cult, a mainstream faith community, or a more informal spiritual setting, it thrives on the abuse of power dynamics, emotional manipulation, psychological trauma, and social isolation. The leaders who perpetrate spiritual abuse prey on the vulnerability of their followers, disguising their actions under the guise of spiritual guidance or divine authority. Recognizing these signs of abuse is the first step toward healing, as it allows individuals to reclaim their voice, break free from the cycle of control, and restore their sense of spiritual autonomy. The journey to freedom begins with understanding the scope and nature of spiritual abuse, as it paves the way for the recovery and renewal that will be explored in the following chapters

Chapter 2

Saints or Narcissists? – Religious Narcissism Unmasked

Introduction:

In the realm of religious communities, faith is often an individual's most intimate connection, the lifeblood of their existence. It shapes their worldviews, influences their decisions, and governs their sense of purpose. It is within this deeply sacred space that the narcissist thrives, cloaked in the guise of spirituality, and often revered as a spiritual leader or guide. From charismatic leaders to seemingly humble spouses and even "faithful" peers, narcissism in religious contexts is deceptively cloaked, hiding its manipulative, self-serving nature behind a mask of righteousness, selflessness, and divinely inspired authority. These figures are not merely manipulating the outward behaviors of others; they are manipulating their faith, emotions, and trust in the divine to maintain control. In this chapter, we will examine the traits of religious narcissists—whether they are leaders, spouses, or "faithful" peers—and how narcissistic abuse thrives under the guise of spirituality. Furthermore, we will explore two essential psychological constructs that enable religious narcissism to endure: the holy superiority complex and spiritual gaslighting.

Traits of Religious Narcissists (Leaders, Spouses, or "Faithful" Peers)

A religious narcissist, whether they occupy a formal leadership position, assume the role of a spouse, or even take on the persona of a deeply devout peer, shares a set of distinct traits that set them apart from genuine spiritual figures. These individuals excel at creating a facade of piety, virtue, and devotion to God, while underneath, they harbor an insatiable need for power, admiration, and control over others. Understanding these traits is key to recognizing narcissistic behavior within spiritual communities.

1. Charisma and Charm: A Mask of Piety

One of the most distinctive traits of a religious narcissist is their charisma. They are magnetic, often drawing people in with their charm, confidence, and persuasive abilities. This is especially true for religious narcissistic leaders, who often present themselves as possessing a special connection with the divine, making their words and actions seem divinely inspired. In smaller faith communities, a narcissistic peer or spouse may also present themselves in a similar way, claiming to be the one with a deeper understanding of scripture, the will of God, or the "correct" spiritual path.

Charisma in these individuals isn't just about outward personality— it's a carefully constructed image. They appear to radiate compassion, humility, and wisdom, traits that are deeply admired in religious contexts. As a result, their influence grows effortlessly. They are positioned as spiritual guides, experts, or even "holy figures" who have the authority to lead others to salvation, making it difficult for their followers to see through the façade. The narcissist often carefully cultivates this persona to keep followers in awe, ensuring they remain emotionally invested and obedient.

2. Self-Centeredness Masquerading as Altruism

At first glance, religious narcissists seem selfless, dedicating their lives to the service of others, or claiming to do so. However, upon closer inspection, their acts of "service" or "sacrifice" are often self-serving. They may use their position of influence to gain admiration, to assert control, or to extract benefits from their followers. What appears to be selflessness is merely a tool to maintain a facade of righteousness and moral superiority.

For example, a religious leader might demand long hours of service or devotion from their followers, while offering little to no reciprocation. At first, these demands may seem reasonable—after all, they are working for the greater good, right? But this constant expectation of sacrifice, under the guise of spiritual growth, is a sign of narcissistic manipulation. Narcissists thrive in environments where others praise their altruism, often with no real intent of benefiting others, but solely to fill their own egos and bolster their status within the community.

Similarly, a spouse or peer exhibiting narcissistic traits might frame their needs or desires as deeply spiritual in nature, positioning themselves as virtuous in their actions or requests. The narcissist expects others to see their actions as noble, demanding adulation and thanks for every "selfless" act they undertake, regardless of the impact it has on others.

3. The Need for Adoration and Constant Validation

Religious narcissists demand constant validation and admiration. This manifests in multiple ways—be it through the worship of followers, the acknowledgement of their piety, or the incessant praise of their wisdom. In a faith community, the narcissist is seen not just as a leader but as a vessel of divine insight and authority. The follower is made to believe that their faith is incomplete or faulty unless it is directed towards reverence for the narcissist.

This need for adoration is not just about attention—it's about power. The narcissist controls the community by ensuring that their self-worth is validated at all times. They may subtly or overtly demand praise and recognition, making their followers feel spiritually indebted to them for spiritual or personal guidance. This manipulation of praise is what sustains the narcissist's ego—without it, their entire identity may collapse, as it is built entirely on the approval and devotion of others.

4. Lack of Empathy and Exploitation of Others

Another key trait of religious narcissists is a complete lack of empathy. While they may appear compassionate and understanding on the surface, underneath they are often indifferent or even callous to the emotional, spiritual, or physical needs of others. They exploit the trust and vulnerability of their followers for personal gain, whether that gain is attention, power, financial resources, or even social standing.

In a religious community, this lack of empathy can manifest in a variety of ways. A narcissistic leader might dismiss the suffering of a member, claiming that their difficulties are due to a lack of faith or obedience. They may offer superficial support—like prayers or comforting words—but fail to engage meaningfully with the actual needs or concerns of others. This dismissal can make followers feel alienated or ashamed, often deepening their dependency on the narcissist for emotional or spiritual support.

For a spouse or peer with narcissistic tendencies, their lack of empathy might be most evident in their relationships. They may present themselves as loving and caring, yet when their partner or peer needs emotional support or comfort, the narcissist may respond with indifference or frustration. These individuals rarely show genuine concern for the feelings of others unless it serves their own interests.

How Narcissistic Abuse Thrives Under the Guise of Spirituality

Narcissistic abuse in a religious context is particularly insidious because it is often disguised as divine wisdom, spiritual guidance, or even the will of God. The narcissist's manipulation is hidden behind a veil of holiness, making it difficult for followers to discern the abuse. Spirituality becomes not a tool for personal growth and connection with God but a mechanism for control and exploitation.

1. Spiritual Authority as a Weapon

The primary tool of the religious narcissist is the manipulation of spiritual authority. A narcissistic leader may claim that their teachings are divinely inspired, positioning themselves as the only person who can interpret God's will. They may assert that their understanding of scripture, tradition, or doctrine is the only valid one, and followers are expected to obey their teachings without question. This assertion of spiritual authority is often grounded in the narcissist's need to control and dominate others, rather than any true desire to guide them in their faith journey.

By cloaking their actions in spiritual language, narcissists create an environment where questioning their authority is not only dangerous but potentially sinful. Followers are conditioned to believe that challenging the leader's wisdom is an affront to God, which places the narcissist in a position of untouchable power. In this scenario, the follower is led to believe that they are spiritually inferior if they feel discomfort, doubt, or a need for independence from the leader's teachings.

2. Spiritual Gaslighting: Distorting Reality for Control

One of the most powerful tools of the religious narcissist is spiritual gaslighting. Gaslighting is a form of psychological manipulation where the narcissist causes the follower to question their own perception of reality. In a religious context, this takes on a spiritual dimension. The narcissist may use scripture, religious texts, or the "will of God" to make their followers doubt their own faith, experiences, or personal understanding of God's teachings.

For example, a narcissistic leader might tell a follower that their doubts or struggles with faith are a sign of sin or spiritual weakness. They may use religious language to confuse the follower, telling them that their spiritual experiences are not authentic or that they are "unworthy" of divine love or blessings. This spiritual manipulation leaves the follower feeling disoriented, uncertain, and dependent on the narcissist for spiritual guidance. Over time, the follower may begin to doubt their own relationship with God, unable to trust their instincts or perceptions of truth.

3. The Holy Superiority Complex

Religious narcissists often possess a "holy superiority complex," where they believe themselves to be the ultimate authority on spiritual matters, far above the rest of the community. This belief manifests in a variety of ways. A religious narcissist might claim to have a unique connection to God, positioning themselves as a spiritual intermediary between their followers and the divine. Their ideas, teachings, and behaviors are seen as beyond reproach, and they are revered as "holy figures" who hold a special status within the faith community.

This sense of superiority serves several purposes. It reinforces the narcissist's ego, allowing them to maintain control over their followers, and it justifies their behavior, no matter how manipulative or abusive. The followers are made to believe that they are spiritually inferior and that their only chance at salvation or enlightenment lies in obedience to the narcissist's teachings and directives. The narcissist exploits this sense of superiority to assert dominance, limit personal autonomy, and maintain a high level of influence over the community.

4. The Cycle of Dependency and Control

Narcissists thrive on control, and religious narcissists are no different. They create a cycle of dependency where their followers believe they are incapable of spiritual growth, guidance, or decision-making without the narcissist's intervention. This dependency is fostered through a mixture of praise, guilt, and manipulation, keeping followers emotionally invested and loyal. Any attempt to break free from this cycle is met with emotional or spiritual repercussions, often framed as punishment or rejection by God.

By continually reinforcing the idea that their followers need them for spiritual fulfillment, the narcissist creates a system of control that is difficult to escape. The follower becomes convinced that their own spiritual journey is incomplete without the narcissist's input, which isolates them from other sources of guidance, support, and truth.

The Holy Superiority Complex and Spiritual Gaslighting

At the heart of narcissistic behavior in religious contexts is the "holy superiority complex," a belief in one's own divinely ordained superiority. Coupled with spiritual gaslighting, this complex allows narcissistic individuals to manipulate their followers on an emotional, psychological, and spiritual level. The narcissist's delusions of grandeur become legitimized through their perceived connection to God, and they use spiritual language to convince others of their inherent superiority.

Spiritual gaslighting, in particular, plays a critical role in maintaining control. By distorting the follower's perception of reality—making them question their own spiritual understanding or experiences—the narcissist creates an environment of confusion, doubt, and emotional distress. This makes it nearly impossible for the follower to break free from the cycle of abuse, as they are convinced that their experiences of doubt or discomfort are wrong, sinful, or misguided.

Conclusion:

Religious narcissism is a pervasive and destructive force that hides behind the sacred and the divine. Whether in the form of a leader, spouse, or peer, narcissists use spirituality to manipulate, control, and exploit others for personal gain. They do so by leveraging their charisma, their self-centeredness masquerading as altruism, and their desperate need for validation to maintain power and influence over their followers. Through spiritual gaslighting and the holy superiority complex, they distort reality, keep followers in a perpetual state of dependence, and exploit their vulnerabilities. In the next chapter, we will explore how to identify these toxic dynamics and begin the process of healing and recovery. Reclaiming one's spiritual independence is possible, but first, we must confront the narcissistic abuse that thrives under the guise of piety.

Chapter 3
The Gospel According to Control – Tactics of Manipulation

Introduction:

In the context of spiritual abuse, manipulation is a central theme, often hidden under the guise of religious righteousness. Religious narcissists and controlling figures use spiritual authority to exert dominance over their followers, distorting the very messages of faith to serve their personal agendas. The tactics of manipulation within these contexts are insidious, feeding on deeply held beliefs, vulnerabilities, and emotional needs to trap individuals into a cycle of dependency and fear. This chapter will explore three of the most potent tactics used by religious abusers: fear, guilt, and shame as weapons; the manipulation of isolation and the "us vs. them" mentality; and the distortion of obedience theology and doctrine. These tactics are not merely psychological tools—they are spiritual weapons designed to maintain control, suppress individuality, and discourage critical thought. Understanding these methods is crucial to recognizing spiritual manipulation and ultimately reclaiming one's spiritual freedom.

Fear, Guilt, and Shame as Weapons

Fear, guilt, and shame are powerful emotions that have been used throughout history as tools of control. In religious contexts, these emotions are frequently weaponized by narcissistic leaders and spiritually abusive individuals to maintain dominance over their followers. These tactics prey on the deepest insecurities, spiritual doubts, and emotional vulnerabilities of individuals, using their fear of spiritual consequences and moral failing to manipulate their behavior.

Fear: The Fear of Damnation or Divine Wrath

Fear is one of the most potent tools in a religious narcissist's arsenal. The fear of eternal damnation or divine punishment is often used as a means to control behavior, silence dissent, and keep individuals obedient to the leader's demands. Religious narcissists often employ a combination of scripture and emotional rhetoric to create an atmosphere of fear. They may warn followers that straying from the leader's teachings or questioning their authority will lead to dire spiritual consequences.

The fear of losing one's salvation or experiencing God's wrath is a deeply powerful motivator. Followers become so consumed by the desire to avoid these imagined consequences that they abandon their personal desires, thoughts, and needs, surrendering themselves entirely to the leader's will. This constant fear often clouds their judgment, making it harder for individuals to recognize manipulation or abuse within the religious framework.

In more extreme cases, narcissistic leaders may escalate the fear to the point of creating a "spiritual panic," where followers believe that they are in constant danger of spiritual ruin. This manufactured fear ensures that the narcissist remains the sole figure of trust and protection.

Followers become dependent on the leader for assurance, even though the leader is the one creating the very fear they seek to alleviate.

Guilt: The Burden of Unworthiness

Guilt is another powerful emotional weapon used by narcissistic religious figures. Guilt trips are often employed to control behavior, making followers feel as though they are falling short of divine expectations. This can take the form of accusations such as, "You are not living up to God's will," or "You are disappointing God by questioning my authority." The language of guilt is designed to make individuals feel that their doubts or questions are a reflection of their spiritual inadequacy.

This tactic operates under the assumption that followers are inherently flawed and need to be constantly reminded of their shortcomings. It keeps them in a state of emotional servitude, constantly striving to meet the narcissist's ever-changing expectations. Those who succumb to the guilt may feel like failures, constantly repenting for perceived sins or flaws, even if these "failures" are based on the narcissist's arbitrary standards.

The manipulator knows how to exploit guilt, creating a vicious cycle in which the follower believes that they can only receive spiritual approval through obedience and submission. Guilt makes followers reluctant to voice their concerns, ask questions, or seek external counsel. Instead, they internalize the idea that they must remain loyal to the narcissistic leader, as only by doing so can they attain redemption or forgiveness.

Shame: The Destruction of Self-Worth

Shame is perhaps the most damaging weapon in the spiritual narcissist's arsenal. While guilt involves the idea of having done something wrong, shame is the belief that *who you are* is wrong—that your very being is flawed or unworthy. Religious narcissists exploit shame by making followers believe that they are not worthy of God's love or salvation unless they comply with the narcissist's demands.

Shame operates through humiliation and self-doubt. A narcissistic leader may manipulate followers into believing that their personal struggles or doubts are evidence of their spiritual failure. Followers may feel that they are defective or unworthy of love because they are not adhering perfectly to the narcissist's interpretation of religious teachings. This destroys self-confidence, making it difficult for individuals to recognize their own worth outside of the narcissist's approval.

The narcissist may then offer conditional love or acceptance, promising followers that they can only experience God's favor or spiritual peace if they fulfill the leader's demands. This constant cycle of shame and false promises creates an environment where the follower's sense of self is entirely dictated by the narcissist's whims. The narcissist becomes the only source of validation, further deepening the emotional control they hold over the individual.

Isolation and "Us vs. Them" Thinking

One of the hallmarks of religious manipulation is the use of isolation as a method to control and manipulate individuals. Isolation serves two

24

primary functions: it disconnects the follower from external sources of support and information, and it strengthens the narcissist's control over the individual's perception of reality. Religious narcissists often manipulate followers into believing that their community is the only true spiritual path, making them feel isolated from the outside world.

Creating a Separate Spiritual Universe

Religious narcissists often create an "us vs. them" mentality that fosters division between the spiritual community and the world at large. They frame outsiders as threats to the truth or salvation, often portraying them as evil, misguided, or spiritually inferior. This "us vs. them" thinking becomes deeply ingrained, making followers view anyone outside the group with suspicion or disdain. The narcissist's word is the only truth, and anything or anyone that contradicts it is dismissed as a danger to spiritual purity.

This mentality can be particularly damaging to individuals who begin to question the narcissist's authority. The narcissist will typically accuse these individuals of being spiritually immature or rebellious, pressuring them to rejoin the community's "correct" path. This creates a sense of alienation, where the follower feels torn between their desire to seek answers and the pressure to remain loyal to the narcissistic figure and their community.

Through this isolation, the narcissist keeps the follower in a state of dependency. They are made to believe that the narcissist is the only person who can provide them with spiritual guidance, and any outside voices or perspectives are labeled as dangerous. This isolation leaves the follower with little to no emotional or intellectual support to challenge the narcissist's control, making it difficult for them to recognize the manipulation at play.

Severing Relationships with Friends and Family

In more extreme cases, narcissistic leaders or abusive spouses will encourage or even demand that followers cut ties with family and friends who are not part of the community or who are seen as "ungodly" or a threat to the spiritual path. This forced separation isolates the individual even further, creating an emotional and social vacuum that only the narcissist can fill.

The isolation tactic also serves to prevent any criticism from being voiced within the community. Without the ability to discuss concerns with trusted outsiders, the follower remains vulnerable to the narcissist's manipulative techniques. In this way, the narcissist creates a tightly controlled environment in which their authority is unchallenged and unquestioned.

Obedience Theology and Distorted Doctrines

Obedience theology refers to the theological stance that absolute obedience to religious authority, often the leader, is a requisite for spiritual salvation or divine favor. This distorted understanding of religious obedience is frequently exploited by narcissistic leaders to maintain control over their followers. The manipulation of obedience theology is one of the most insidious tactics in spiritual abuse because it fundamentally alters the individual's relationship with God, shifting it from one of personal devotion to one of servitude to the narcissist.

The Distortion of Scripture for Control

Religious narcissists often manipulate religious texts or doctrines to justify their abusive behavior and demand complete obedience. They selectively cite verses or teachings that support their agenda while ignoring or distorting others that promote freedom, love, and compassion. For example, a narcissistic leader may emphasize passages that require submission to authority while downplaying those that encourage personal discernment, justice, and equality.

By doing so, they create a religious framework where followers are conditioned to believe that obedience to the leader is not only expected but required by God. They may teach that questioning the leader's directives is equivalent to questioning God's will, thus condemning the individual to spiritual consequences. This turns the leader into a godlike figure whose commands must be followed without question, regardless of how they conflict with the follower's personal beliefs, ethical values, or spiritual growth.

The Manipulation of Faith for Personal Gain

This distorted doctrine of obedience often extends to the narcissist's personal gain. They may demand tithes, services, or other forms of submission, often framing these demands as necessary for spiritual growth or God's blessing. Followers may be told that failing to comply will result in spiritual punishment, loss of blessings, or separation from

God. In extreme cases, the narcissist may even position themselves as the gatekeeper to salvation, making followers believe that their eternal fate is entirely in the hands of the leader's approval.

Conclusion:

The tactics of manipulation employed by religious narcissists—fear, guilt, shame, isolation, and distorted doctrines—are as dangerous as they are effective. They not only manipulate the followers' behavior but distort their relationship with spirituality, faith, and self-worth. These tactics create an environment where questioning the leader's authority becomes nearly impossible and personal freedom is sacrificed at the altar of submission. The emotional and spiritual consequences of these manipulations can be devastating, leaving individuals feeling isolated, unworthy, and dependent on the narcissist for approval and validation.

Recognizing these tactics is the first step in breaking free from spiritual abuse. In the next chapters, we will explore the path to healing, learning to reestablish personal autonomy, reconnect with one's faith in a healthy way, and rebuild a sense of spiritual authenticity that is not tainted by the abuse of power. Only by confronting these manipulative practices can individuals begin to reclaim their spiritual and emotional independence.

Chapter 4

The Devout Trauma – Signs You've Been Spiritually Abused

Introduction:

Spiritual abuse is a hidden wound—one that doesn't always leave visible scars but can leave deep emotional, psychological, and even spiritual damage. For those who experience it, the effects can be subtle at first, creeping into their thoughts, emotions, and sense of self, often disguised as divine authority, righteousness, or spiritual growth. Over time, however, the impact becomes undeniable. The chronic anxiety, self-doubt, and moral confusion that arise from spiritual manipulation can erode a person's peace, leaving them unsure of themselves, their faith, and their relationship with God. Devotion, once a source of strength, can turn into a prison that isolates, diminishes, and distorts the very essence of who they are. In this chapter, we will explore the signs of spiritual abuse—those feelings of anxiety, self-doubt, and moral confusion—and how they manifest in the lives of those who have been spiritually manipulated. We will also examine how a loss of self-worth, disguised as "humility," can leave a person feeling trapped in their devotion, and how to recognize when devotion to a faith or a leader feels less like a calling and more like a cage.

Chronic Anxiety, Self-Doubt, and Moral Confusion

One of the most debilitating effects of spiritual abuse is the profound sense of anxiety, self-doubt, and moral confusion it causes. Individuals who have been spiritually manipulated often find themselves in a constant state of emotional turmoil. The inner peace that faith is supposed to provide is replaced by a nagging sense of insecurity and fear—fear of not being good enough, fear of making mistakes, or fear of facing divine judgment. This anxiety can manifest in various ways, including emotional exhaustion, physical symptoms of stress, and an overwhelming sense of disorientation about one's faith and life choices.

Chronic Anxiety: The Fear of Spiritual Failure

For those who have experienced spiritual abuse, anxiety becomes a constant companion. The narcissistic or controlling figures in the religious setting often use fear to manipulate followers, convincing them that failure to comply with certain expectations or demands could result in spiritual punishment or even eternal damnation. This fear is not only of punishment from the leader but also of God's disapproval.

In many spiritual abuse situations, followers are taught that their worth is intrinsically tied to their ability to adhere to the leader's teachings or religious dogma. Every misstep or deviation from the prescribed path is seen as a failure, leading to a heightened sense of anxiety. The fear of making a wrong decision, saying the wrong thing, or not living up to the leader's expectations can feel paralyzing. This pervasive anxiety affects not just their spiritual life but their personal and professional lives, as they constantly strive to meet impossible standards set by the manipulative authority figures around them.

Self-Doubt: The Erosion of Spiritual Confidence

As a result of spiritual abuse, self-doubt becomes pervasive. Narcissistic leaders or spiritual manipulators often undermine their followers' ability to trust their own spiritual experiences or convictions. Followers are made to believe that their doubts are sinful or a sign of spiritual immaturity. In some cases, the narcissist may even use gaslighting techniques to make the individual question their own understanding of God, scripture, or spiritual truth.

This leads to a state of perpetual self-doubt, where followers second-guess their decisions, their beliefs, and their ability to connect with God. They may feel disconnected from their own spirituality, unsure of whether their faith is genuine or whether it has been tainted by manipulation. Self-doubt creates a dangerous cycle of dependency on the narcissistic leader, as followers feel they can't trust their own judgment or relationship with God. In this state of confusion, they often turn to the abuser for guidance, only deepening their sense of helplessness and uncertainty.

Moral Confusion: The Battle Between Right and Wrong

Moral confusion is another hallmark of spiritual abuse. The narcissistic leader often distorts religious teachings and manipulates moral principles to justify their actions and demands. This can leave followers confused about what is right or wrong, especially when the leader's behavior contradicts the very values they claim to uphold.

For example, a leader might demand excessive loyalty or even financial support from their followers, presenting these actions as acts of divine obedience. Followers, having been conditioned to obey without question, may struggle with the moral implications of such demands, unsure if they are truly following God's will or simply complying with the manipulator's desires. This confusion can bleed into other areas of life, making it difficult for individuals to make clear, ethical decisions and causing an ongoing moral struggle that can erode their peace of mind.

The moral confusion caused by spiritual abuse can make individuals feel as though they are constantly walking on a tightrope, unsure of which path is righteous and which will lead to spiritual ruin. This uncertainty often fuels the cycle of dependence on the narcissistic leader, as the abuser is the only figure offering clarity, even if it's distorted and self-serving.

Loss of Self-Worth Cloaked in "Humility"

In many cases of spiritual abuse, the loss of self-worth is masked by the false guise of humility. Narcissistic leaders or abusers often frame their demands for loyalty, obedience, and submission as spiritual virtues. They present their control over followers as a form of Godly authority or divine discipline, making it appear as though the follower's humility is the path to spiritual fulfillment. This is a dangerous distortion of humility, which, in the context of spiritual abuse, becomes a tool of control and submission rather than a genuine expression of reverence or selflessness.

The False Virtue of Humility

Humility, as taught by spiritual abusers, is not about embracing modesty or self-awareness. It is about suppressing personal needs, desires, and beliefs in favor of the leader's or the group's demands. The narcissist redefines humility as unquestioning obedience, making the follower believe that to be humble is to surrender their personal identity, desires, and autonomy. This version of humility strips the individual of their self-worth, forcing them to believe that their value lies solely in their submission to the leader or religious system.

As a result, the follower begins to see themselves as small, insignificant, and unworthy of recognition unless they are serving the narcissist's agenda. They may feel ashamed of their own desires, talents, or independent thoughts, believing that to express them would be prideful or sinful. The follower may even come to believe that self-sacrifice for the leader is the ultimate form of devotion and spiritual maturity, further diminishing their sense of self and increasing their emotional dependency on the abuser.

The Internalized Message of Unworthiness

The narcissistic manipulator often reinforces the message of unworthiness, telling followers that they are flawed, sinful, or incapable of achieving spiritual success on their own. This internalized message chips away at the follower's sense of self-worth, leaving them with feelings of inadequacy and a constant need for validation from the leader. Even when they perform good deeds, make spiritual progress, or demonstrate positive changes, they are made to feel that it is never enough. The narcissist may downplay their accomplishments, making the follower feel unworthy of love or recognition unless they give more—more time, more loyalty, more sacrifice.

This loss of self-worth can take a toll on the follower's emotional and mental health. They may feel trapped in a cycle of striving for perfection, believing that their value is contingent on meeting the leader's expectations. Even when they attempt to take steps toward independence, the fear of rejection or punishment by the leader or the community can pull them back into submission, reinforcing the idea that they are nothing without the leader's approval.

When Devotion Feels Like a Prison

One of the most insidious aspects of spiritual abuse is how devotion, once a source of strength and peace, becomes a form of emotional and spiritual imprisonment. What was initially a genuine desire to follow God and serve others becomes twisted into a suffocating obligation to meet the narcissist's needs and demands. The follower, who once felt liberated by their faith, begins to feel trapped, unable to escape the constant cycle of expectations and fear.

The Burden of Unfulfilled Expectations

Devotion to a leader or religious system that promotes spiritual abuse becomes a heavy burden. The follower is constantly reminded of their shortcomings, told they need to do more, be more, and give more. The narcissist uses religious language to justify these demands, claiming that it is for the follower's spiritual growth, yet the follower's personal needs and growth are neglected. Instead of nurturing a relationship with God, the follower is forced into a transactional relationship with the narcissist, where every act of devotion is in service of the leader's agenda.

As the follower becomes more entangled in this cycle, their faith begins to feel less like a relationship with the divine and more like a prison. What was once a source of peace and joy becomes a source of anxiety and distress. The follower may feel that if they step out of line, their entire spiritual existence will collapse. They may be unable to separate their devotion to God from their devotion to the manipulative figure who has taken control of their spiritual journey.

The Desire for Freedom: Breaking the Chains

The desire for spiritual freedom is often suppressed, as the follower fears the consequences of questioning or leaving the religious system. Even if they begin to recognize the manipulation, the fear of divine punishment or social ostracization may prevent them from taking action. The follower may rationalize their suffering, believing that it is part of God's plan, or that they are somehow "unworthy" of true spiritual freedom.

However, as the follower begins to heal and break free from the prison of spiritual abuse, they can reclaim their faith in a way that is authentic and liberating. Healing from spiritual abuse requires confronting the pain, challenging the distorted teachings, and rediscovering a relationship with God that is not defined by fear, shame, or control.

Conclusion:

The signs of spiritual abuse—chronic anxiety, self-doubt, moral confusion, the loss of self-worth disguised as humility, and the experience of devotion as a prison—are all symptoms of a much deeper wound. These emotional and spiritual scars can be difficult to recognize, especially when they are so deeply intertwined with one's faith. However, by acknowledging these signs, individuals can begin the process of healing, reclaiming their spiritual autonomy, and finding freedom from the grip of spiritual manipulation. The journey to recovery involves rediscovering a faith that is not rooted in fear, guilt, or shame, but in love, authenticity, and self-worth. In the next chapters, we will explore how individuals can rebuild their sense of self and their connection to the divine, free from the toxic influence of spiritual abuse.

PART II
BREAKING THE SPELL –
RECLAIMING YOUR VOICE

Chapter 5

From Sacred Silence to Speaking Truth – Telling Your Story

Introduction:

For many survivors of spiritual abuse, the journey from silence to speaking out is fraught with emotional, psychological, and spiritual challenges. For years, they have endured manipulation, control, and emotional harm, often in the name of faith or spiritual growth. The very nature of spiritual abuse—rooted in trust, authority, and belief—makes it incredibly difficult to find a voice, let alone speak truthfully about the abuse they've experienced. Speaking up about spiritual abuse requires more than just the courage to break free; it necessitates the bravery to confront the spiritual lies and emotional scars that have been deeply embedded in their hearts. This chapter will explore why survivors struggle to speak up, the power of naming the abuse as a step toward healing, and how to find safe ways and supportive people to share their stories.

Why Survivors Struggle to Speak Up

Survivors of spiritual abuse often find themselves in a complex psychological and emotional web that makes it difficult to speak out, even long after the abuse has ended. This silence is not merely a result of fear or shame; it is often the product of years of manipulation, gaslighting, and emotional conditioning that tells the survivor their voice does not matter, or worse, that they are the ones in the wrong.

The Fear of Repercussions

One of the primary reasons survivors struggle to speak up is the fear of consequences—both from the narcissistic abuser and the community. In many cases, the narcissistic leader or spiritual abuser is in a position of authority, and their followers are conditioned to view them as divinely chosen or infallible. Challenging the leader's authority or speaking out about their abuse can feel like a direct challenge to God's will or a threat to one's spiritual standing. This fear of divine retribution or punishment is deeply ingrained, especially when the narcissist uses scripture or religious teachings to justify their abusive actions.

Moreover, in tightly-knit religious communities, speaking up can lead to social ostracization, public shaming, or excommunication. The fear of being labeled as rebellious, sinful, or unfaithful often silences survivors, even when they know that what they endured was wrong. The fear of being abandoned by friends, family, and the larger religious group can make the idea of speaking out feel overwhelming.

Internalized Guilt and Shame

Another reason survivors hesitate to speak up is the internalized guilt and shame that often result from spiritual abuse. Narcissistic leaders and manipulators often use shame as a tool to control their followers. They may convince survivors that their doubts, struggles, or questions are signs of sin or spiritual inadequacy. Over time, these messages become internalized, making the survivor feel as though they are somehow responsible for the abuse they experienced.

Survivors may believe that they are weak or lacking in faith for not submitting to the leader's authority. They may feel ashamed for questioning their faith or for not being able to "just trust" and "obey." This internalized guilt creates a barrier to speaking up, as survivors may fear they are somehow complicit in the abuse or that their complaints are invalid. Even after leaving the abusive environment, these feelings can persist, making it difficult to find the courage to speak their truth.

The Spiritual Disconnect: Doubting One's Own Voice

For those who have experienced spiritual abuse, there is often a deep, lingering sense of spiritual confusion. The very foundations of their faith have been manipulated, and their relationship with God has been distorted. Many survivors struggle with doubts about their own beliefs, questioning whether what they experienced was truly abuse or if it was just part of a "God-ordained" path. In some cases, survivors may even doubt their own perceptions, having been gaslighted for so long by the abuser that they are uncertain whether they were truly harmed.

This confusion can lead to a feeling of disconnection from one's spiritual self. When someone is unable to trust their own faith or the authenticity of their experiences, speaking up about the abuse becomes an emotionally daunting task. The fear of further invalidating their spiritual identity can keep survivors silent, even when they yearn for the truth to be heard.

The Fear of Not Being Believed

A significant barrier to speaking up for many survivors is the fear of not being believed or having their experiences minimized. In religious settings, abuse can often be dismissed as a misunderstanding or even as divine discipline. Spiritual abusers frequently position themselves as the final authority on matters of faith, and their followers may be conditioned to believe that they are the ones in the wrong. The fear of not being taken seriously, especially in the context of religious manipulation, can prevent survivors from speaking out. They may fear that their story will be dismissed as a momentary lapse in judgment or that they will be blamed for the situation.

The potential for victim-blaming or minimizing the abuse can be especially painful, as it invalidates the survivor's experience and reinforces the shame they may already feel. This creates a silencing effect that keeps the survivor from finding their voice or seeking support from others who might understand their pain.

The Healing Power of Naming the Abuse

Naming the abuse is a transformative and necessary step in the healing process. When survivors finally speak out about the abuse they've experienced, they begin to reclaim their sense of agency, dignity, and spiritual autonomy. The act of naming the abuse is powerful because it allows survivors to confront the manipulation and control they endured and to separate their personal experience from the lies they were told.

Reclaiming Personal Truth

By giving the abuse a name, survivors begin to reassert control over their narrative. Spiritual abuse often involves the narcissist creating an alternate version of reality, where the survivor's experiences are invalidated or distorted. Naming the abuse is a way for the survivor to say, "This happened, and it was wrong." It is a way of claiming their truth, their emotions, and their personal journey, free from the distortions and manipulations of the abuser.

Naming the abuse also helps survivors separate their faith from the abusive actions of the leader or community. It allows them to begin the process of healing from the trauma of abuse while still maintaining the possibility of a healthy, authentic spiritual life. By acknowledging the harm they endured, survivors can begin to heal from the emotional and spiritual scars that the abuse left behind.

Releasing Shame and Guilt

Naming the abuse also serves as a powerful antidote to the shame and guilt that survivors may feel. Spiritual abusers often use shame as a tool to manipulate their followers, making them feel as though they are spiritually inadequate, sinful, or unworthy. When survivors name the abuse, they take the first step toward releasing the shame that has been imposed upon them. It is an affirmation that the abuse was not their fault, and that they are not responsible for the manipulations they endured.

By sharing their story, survivors can also find the courage to forgive themselves for staying in the abusive situation, if that is part of their healing process. Naming the abuse is an act of self-compassion—it is a way of saying, "I was hurt, but I am not to blame."

Safe Ways and Safe People to Share With

For many survivors, finding the right people and places to share their story is crucial to their healing process. It is important to approach this step with caution, as not all environments or individuals are supportive or safe. The goal is to find spaces where survivors can speak their truth without fear of judgment, retaliation, or further abuse.

Therapy and Counseling

One of the safest places to begin speaking about spiritual abuse is with a trained therapist or counselor who specializes in trauma and abuse. A mental health professional can offer a safe, non-judgmental space for survivors to process their experiences, validate their feelings, and work through the complex emotions that often accompany spiritual abuse. Therapy can also help survivors rebuild their sense of self-worth, reconnect with their spiritual identity, and develop healthy coping mechanisms for dealing with the aftermath of abuse.

Support Groups for Survivors of Spiritual Abuse

Support groups specifically for survivors of spiritual abuse can provide an invaluable space for survivors to share their stories with others who have had similar experiences. These groups create a sense of solidarity, helping survivors feel understood and validated. In these groups, survivors can exchange advice, share their healing journeys, and find emotional support from others who have walked the same path.

Support groups offer the added benefit of being a space where survivors can talk freely, knowing that others can relate to their pain and struggles.

Trusted Friends and Mentors

It's also important for survivors to seek out safe, trusted individuals in their personal lives—friends, family members, or mentors—who can provide emotional support. However, not all people will understand the complexities of spiritual abuse. It is essential to choose individuals who are compassionate, open-minded, and non-judgmental. The survivor should look for people who will listen without rushing to offer solutions, who will validate their feelings, and who will hold space for their emotional and spiritual healing.

Online Communities

For some, sharing their story online with anonymous communities or blogs can also be a way to speak out safely. Many online platforms offer survivor communities where people can share their stories without fear of immediate personal repercussions. These platforms can provide an outlet for expression and connection with others who are healing from similar experiences. However, it is essential to approach online sharing with caution, as some platforms may not be entirely supportive or secure.

Conclusion:

The journey from sacred silence to speaking the truth is one of the most transformative steps in healing from spiritual abuse. It requires immense courage, but the act of naming the abuse and reclaiming one's voice is a powerful declaration of independence and recovery. Survivors can free themselves from the emotional and spiritual constraints of the abuse, releasing shame and guilt and reclaiming their personal truth. Speaking out can lead to deeper healing, emotional release, and spiritual restoration, but it must be done in a safe, supportive environment. By finding the right people and spaces to share their story, survivors can begin the process of healing from the trauma of spiritual abuse and move toward a future where their voice, their faith, and their identity are their own.

Chapter 6

Deconstruct Without Despair – Faith, Doubt, and Freedom

Introduction:

The process of deconstructing one's faith is often a deeply emotional, complex, and at times, isolating journey. For many survivors of spiritual abuse, the very act of questioning their beliefs can feel like unraveling the very fabric of their identity. The idea of faith can be synonymous with security, purpose, and connection to something greater. So when the foundation of those beliefs begins to shift, it can be disorienting and even terrifying. The fear of losing one's faith altogether, or feeling disconnected from the divine, can make this process feel like a journey toward spiritual collapse rather than freedom.

However, deconstruction—the process of critically re-examining beliefs and spiritual structures—is not inherently destructive. It does not have to lead to the loss of faith, but rather, it can pave the way for a more personal, resilient, and authentic spirituality. This chapter will explore how to navigate the delicate balance between faith and doubt, the difference between deconstructing faith and losing it entirely, and how to ask difficult questions without falling apart. Most importantly, we will discuss how to rebuild a spirituality that is rooted in personal authenticity, freedom, and strength, and how deconstruction can ultimately lead to spiritual renewal rather than despair.

Understanding Faith Deconstruction vs. Loss of Faith

It's essential to differentiate between the process of faith deconstruction and the loss of faith. While they may seem similar on the surface, they are vastly different in their outcomes and implications. Faith deconstruction is a deliberate, intentional process of questioning, reevaluating, and reassessing religious beliefs and practices that may no longer resonate with one's personal experience or understanding. It is often driven by the need to align one's spirituality with their truth, not out of rejection of faith itself but in pursuit of a deeper, more authentic relationship with the divine.

On the other hand, the loss of faith often occurs as a result of emotional or spiritual harm, such as spiritual abuse, trauma, or deep disillusionment. It is characterized by a sense of spiritual disconnection, apathy, or an abandonment of belief altogether. The loss of faith is often marked by despair, confusion, and a profound sense of loss. This is different from deconstruction because the latter involves critical thinking and the desire to explore new avenues for spiritual growth, while the former often comes from a place of profound disillusionment or pain.

Faith Deconstruction: A Path to Personal Truth

Faith deconstruction is not necessarily an end but a beginning. It is the process of peeling back the layers of inherited beliefs, cultural expectations, and institutional doctrines to uncover what is truly meaningful and authentic for the individual. It allows for the possibility of moving away from rigid, dogmatic understandings of faith and embracing a more flexible, personal, and lived experience of spirituality.

Deconstruction can involve questioning long-held religious beliefs—such as the nature of God, the role of scripture, the purpose of suffering, or the practices of a particular religious tradition. For someone who has experienced spiritual abuse, deconstruction is often a necessary step toward healing, as it helps the individual separate their personal spiritual experience from the manipulation and control they endured. Deconstruction is not about rejecting faith but about re-claiming it from a place of empowerment and self-awareness.

It's important to recognize that deconstruction can be a painful process, but it doesn't have to result in a loss of faith. Instead, it can lead to spiritual liberation and a more profound understanding of one's relationship with the divine, one that is no longer defined by fear, shame, or manipulation.

The Loss of Faith: Disillusionment and Disconnect

For those who experience spiritual abuse or deep disillusionment, the loss of faith can feel like an insurmountable void. The concepts that once provided comfort, meaning, and purpose may no longer resonate. Instead of the faith being a source of guidance and support, it may feel like a source of pain, confusion, and betrayal. This experience can often lead to a feeling of abandonment by God or the divine, and for some, it may feel as though all their previous beliefs were false or illusory.

While faith deconstruction is about reclaiming spiritual agency, the loss of faith often involves a sense of being spiritually adrift, uncertain, and disconnected. For survivors of spiritual abuse, the loss of faith may feel like the loss of identity itself, as the religious community and practices were often deeply entwined with their sense of self. This is where deconstruction can offer a way forward. Rather than succumbing to despair or giving up on spirituality altogether, survivors can use deconstruction as a tool for transformation. By consciously choosing to reconstruct their beliefs—without the influence of toxic, manipulative systems—they can begin to rebuild their faith on their terms.

How to Question Without Falling Apart

The process of questioning one's faith can feel destabilizing, particularly when so much of a person's identity is tied to religious beliefs. But questioning doesn't have to lead to emotional or spiritual collapse; it can be a vital part of growth and healing. The key is to approach the process with patience, compassion, and self-awareness.

Create Emotional Space for Reflection

The first step in questioning without falling apart is to give yourself emotional space. Spiritual deconstruction requires time to reflect, ask difficult questions, and allow yourself to sit with uncertainty. This is not a process to rush through, and it's important to approach it with kindness toward yourself. Too often, survivors of spiritual abuse feel pressured to resolve their doubts quickly, but genuine healing and growth take time.

Give yourself permission to not have all the answers immediately and to explore different possibilities without judgment.

Acknowledge that it's okay to feel confused, anxious, or even angry during this process. These emotions are a natural response to the upheaval of reexamining your faith. It's important to create a space where you can feel these emotions without feeling guilty or ashamed for questioning. Spirituality should not be a source of further suffering, but a wellspring of peace and growth.

Find a Supportive Environment for Exploration

Deconstructing faith without falling apart also requires the presence of safe and supportive environments. It is difficult to question your beliefs in isolation, especially if you have been spiritually manipulated or abused. Surrounding yourself with empathetic, open-minded individuals who encourage your exploration—without rushing to offer answers—is essential.

This might involve finding a therapist who specializes in spiritual trauma or abuse, connecting with others who have gone through similar experiences, or joining a group that encourages open, nonjudgmental dialogue about faith. These spaces provide validation, comfort, and a sense of shared experience that can alleviate the feelings of loneliness that often accompany spiritual questioning.

In these supportive environments, you can share your doubts and ask questions freely, knowing that you are not being judged or pressured to conform to any particular belief system. This sense of support will allow you to navigate the complexity of deconstructing faith without feeling overwhelmed or abandoned.

Embrace the Paradox of Uncertainty

One of the most challenging aspects of deconstructing faith is learning to live with uncertainty. Spiritual abuse and dogmatic belief systems often encourage a black-and-white view of faith, where there is a "right" and "wrong" way to believe, and anything outside of that is seen as dangerous or wrong. As you begin to deconstruct, it's important to accept that uncertainty does not equate to weakness or a loss of direction. In fact, uncertainty can be a sign of growth—a willingness to explore new possibilities without clinging to rigid frameworks.

Embrace the paradox of not having all the answers and living with ambiguity. This is not a loss of faith; it is a dynamic, evolving relationship with your beliefs. It allows room for growth, learning, and spiritual depth. Instead of seeing uncertainty as something to fear, begin to view it as an opportunity for deeper connection with the divine, yourself, and others. The ability to live with uncertainty means freeing yourself from the need for certainty to validate your spirituality.

Building a Personal, Resilient Spirituality

As you begin to deconstruct your faith, the ultimate goal is to build a personal, resilient spirituality that aligns with your authentic self. This spirituality is not bound by institutional dogma or external control but is deeply rooted in personal experience, inner truth, and freedom. Building this kind of spirituality involves reconnecting with the divine on your terms and redefining what it means to be spiritually whole.

Trust Yourself and Your Intuition

A resilient spirituality begins with trusting yourself and your intuition. Survivors of spiritual abuse often struggle with self-doubt, as their own voices have been suppressed or ignored. One of the first steps in rebuilding a personal spirituality is learning to trust your inner wisdom again. You may find that the voice you once doubted or suppressed is the very source of guidance you need moving forward.

Trusting yourself means rejecting the notion that only an external authority can define your spiritual path. It means acknowledging that you have the capacity to discern truth, make decisions, and find spiritual meaning without needing validation from anyone but yourself.

Explore Spirituality Beyond Dogma

Building a resilient spirituality also involves letting go of rigid dogma and embracing a more flexible approach to faith. This might include exploring different spiritual traditions, reading texts that resonate with your soul, or engaging in practices that foster connection and inner peace, such as meditation, mindfulness, or nature walks. The goal is not to replace one set of beliefs with another, but to allow for spiritual practices and understandings that nourish you as an individual.

Resilient spirituality is about finding practices that help you reconnect with your sense of peace, purpose, and connection to the divine, free from the constraints of harmful religious systems. It's about discovering what makes you feel whole—whether that involves prayer, art, service, community, or solitude—and embracing it wholeheartedly.

Honor Your Own Journey

Finally, building a resilient spirituality means honoring your own journey. It is not a linear process, and there is no "right" way to approach it. Each person's path is unique, shaped by their experiences, beliefs, and inner wisdom. Allow yourself the space to grow, explore, and evolve, free from judgment or comparison. Your journey is yours alone, and it is worthy of respect and love.

Conclusion:

Deconstructing one's faith is a courageous, transformative process that holds the potential for deep spiritual renewal and personal empowerment. By understanding the difference between faith deconstruction and the loss of faith, learning how to question beliefs without falling apart, and building a personal, resilient spirituality, survivors of spiritual abuse can reclaim their spiritual autonomy. Rather than spiraling into despair, the deconstruction process can lead to a more authentic, empowered, and liberating connection to the divine. As you navigate this journey, remember that faith is not a static, unchanging concept but a dynamic, evolving relationship that can be redefined and rebuilt on your terms.

Chapter 7

Boundaries Aren't Sinful – Learning to Say No to Spiritual Bullies

Introduction:

Spiritual abuse thrives in environments where boundaries are either nonexistent or systematically disregarded. In many religious contexts, individuals are taught that the highest form of devotion is complete submission—submission to God, to church leaders, and to the expectations of a spiritual community. While submission in faith is a virtue, when it is exploited to the point of eroding personal autonomy, it becomes a dangerous tool for control. Spiritual bullies—whether they are leaders, peers, or community members—use this mindset to manipulate, dominate, and control others, making it difficult for individuals to assert their boundaries without feeling guilty, sinful, or unworthy.

Learning to set emotional, physical, and spiritual boundaries is an essential step in reclaiming one's autonomy and healing from spiritual abuse. Boundaries are not a rejection of faith; rather, they are a way of protecting your emotional and spiritual well-being. In this chapter, we will explore how to set healthy boundaries, differentiate between genuine faithfulness and people-pleasing behavior, and employ techniques to assert your autonomy in the face of spiritual bullies. Recognizing that boundaries are not sinful, but rather an act of self-care and self-respect, is crucial to reclaiming control over your life and your relationship with God.

Setting Emotional, Physical, and Spiritual Boundaries

Boundaries are essential for maintaining healthy relationships and a sense of personal well-being. For survivors of spiritual abuse, setting boundaries is a critical part of the healing process. However, many individuals who have been manipulated by spiritual bullies may find it difficult to recognize or enforce boundaries due to the conditioning they have undergone. Below are the types of boundaries that need to be established, along with practical steps for creating and maintaining them.

Emotional Boundaries: Protecting Your Inner World

Emotional boundaries are about protecting your emotional well-being. They involve recognizing and respecting your feelings, needs, and limits, and not allowing others to manipulate or invalidate your emotional state. In spiritually abusive environments, leaders or peers may dismiss your emotions, label your feelings as sinful, or pressure you to suppress them for the sake of the community or leader's agenda. These emotional manipulations can leave you feeling confused, invalidated, and emotionally drained.

To set emotional boundaries, it is important to:

1. **Recognize Your Emotions**: Start by tuning into your emotions and acknowledging how you feel, whether it's anger, sadness, frustration, or confusion. Validate your feelings as legitimate, rather than dismissing them as wrong or sinful.

2. **Limit Emotional Exposure**: If someone consistently triggers negative emotions or manipulates you emotionally, it's okay to limit your exposure to them. This may mean taking breaks from the religious community or avoiding individuals who have a pattern of emotional manipulation.

3. **Communicate Your Needs**: When necessary, express your emotional needs to others. This could mean saying, "I need space to process my thoughts" or "I don't feel comfortable discussing that topic right now." Learn to communicate your emotional limits without guilt or shame.

4. **Practice Self-Compassion**: Setting emotional boundaries is a form of self-respect. Practice kindness and patience with yourself, especially if you've been conditioned to disregard your emotions. Self-compassion reinforces your right to emotional safety and health.

Physical Boundaries: Protecting Your Body and Space

Physical boundaries are about protecting your physical body and personal space. In abusive spiritual environments, physical boundaries may be ignored or violated—whether through unwelcome touch, excessive demands for time and energy, or pressures to comply with group rituals or activities that feel uncomfortable. These violations can create feelings of powerlessness and violation, making it essential to reclaim control over your body and personal space.

To set physical boundaries, you should:

1. **Recognize Your Right to Personal Space**: Understand that your physical body and space are yours alone, and you have the right to say "no" when someone invades them. Whether it's declining a hug, walking away from a conversation, or choosing to leave a situation, asserting your physical boundaries is an act of self-care.

2. **Prioritize Rest and Self-Care**: In spiritually abusive environments, individuals are often pushed to prioritize service to others over their own physical health. Learn to say no to excessive demands that jeopardize your well-being. Taking time for rest, relaxation, and recreation is essential to maintaining healthy physical boundaries.

3. **Set Time Boundaries**: Beyond physical space, time is also a precious resource that needs protection. If the religious community or spiritual leaders are demanding excessive time commitments, learn to establish boundaries regarding your availability. It's okay to say no to volunteering for every event or activity, especially if it's draining or goes against your personal needs.

4. **Use Non-Verbal Cues**: If you feel uncomfortable in a situation, use non-verbal cues to set boundaries. This might include stepping back, avoiding eye contact, or simply walking away from an interaction that feels invasive.

Spiritual Boundaries: Protecting Your Relationship with God

Spiritual boundaries are perhaps the most difficult to set, especially in religious environments where obedience and submission are often seen as virtues. However, protecting your spiritual well-being and relationship with God is essential to healing from spiritual abuse. Spiritual bullies often demand unquestioning obedience or manipulate spiritual practices to serve their own agenda. Setting spiritual boundaries involves reclaiming your right to define and cultivate your own relationship with the divine, free from external control.

To set spiritual boundaries, consider these steps:

1. **Question What Doesn't Serve You**: Recognize that not all spiritual practices, teachings, or expectations are healthy or life-giving. Question teachings that leave you feeling spiritually stifled, shameful, or disconnected from your true self. It's okay to challenge religious beliefs or practices that no longer resonate with your experience of God or spirituality.

2. **Choose Your Own Spiritual Practices**: Find spiritual practices that nourish you—whether it's prayer, meditation, nature walks, journaling, or simply quiet contemplation. These practices should reflect your authentic spiritual journey, not a set of rigid rules or expectations imposed by others.

3. **Disengage from Toxic Spiritual Influences**: If a leader or community continues to manipulate your spirituality, it's okay to disengage. This might mean stepping away from a church or

religious group that is harmful or no longer aligns with your beliefs. Reclaiming your spirituality means taking back the authority to choose where and how you worship.

4. **Establish Your Own Faith Identity**: Take time to explore and define your own beliefs and spiritual identity, free from the pressures of toxic spiritual systems. This process of spiritual self-discovery can be empowering, as it allows you to create a faith that is rooted in your values and experiences.

Differentiating Faithfulness from People-Pleasing

One of the key aspects of spiritual abuse is the blurring of the line between genuine faithfulness to God and the desire to please others—particularly spiritual leaders or communities. Spiritual bullies often manipulate individuals into thinking that their worth is measured by how much they can sacrifice, obey, and please others. People-pleasing behavior, when driven by fear of rejection or punishment, can be detrimental to one's spiritual and emotional health.

Faithfulness to God vs. People-Pleasing

Faithfulness to God is rooted in a relationship built on love, trust, and authenticity. It is an expression of personal devotion and a desire to align with divine truth. People-pleasing, on the other hand, stems from a desire to gain approval, avoid conflict, or fear punishment. People-pleasing often requires suppressing one's own needs, desires, and beliefs to conform to the expectations of others.

To differentiate between faithfulness and people-pleasing, ask yourself:

1. **Is this action motivated by love for God or fear of rejection?** True faithfulness is motivated by love, not fear. If your decisions are driven by a desire to avoid punishment, rejection, or disappointment, you may be engaging in people-pleasing behavior.

2. **Am I sacrificing my integrity to please others?** Faithfulness to God aligns with your personal integrity and values. If you are compromising your authentic self to gain approval from others, it may indicate that people-pleasing has taken hold.

3. **Is this decision nurturing or draining my spirit?** Faithfulness to God should be life-giving and empowering. If your spiritual practices or obligations are draining you emotionally, spiritually, or physically, it may be a sign that people-pleasing is taking precedence over genuine devotion.

Techniques to Assert Your Autonomy

Asserting your autonomy in the face of spiritual bullies requires both inner strength and practical techniques for setting boundaries and protecting your sense of self. Below are some strategies for asserting your autonomy while navigating spiritual abuse and reclaiming your personal power.

1. Practice Saying "No"

Learning to say no is a critical skill in the recovery process from spiritual abuse. Start by saying no to small requests, such as attending an event you don't feel comfortable with, or offering help when you are stretched too thin. Over time, saying no will become easier and will help you reclaim control over your time, energy, and emotional resources.

2. Use "I" Statements

When asserting boundaries, use "I" statements to express your needs. For example, say, "I am not comfortable with that," or "I need to take a break from this commitment." This frames the boundary as a personal need rather than an accusation, making it easier to communicate without feeling defensive or guilty.

3. Expect Resistance

It's important to acknowledge that spiritual bullies or manipulative figures may resist your boundaries, especially if they are used to controlling you. Be prepared for pushback, and stay firm in your resolve. Remember that your boundaries are valid and necessary for your well-being.

4. Reaffirm Your Right to Personal Space

Remind yourself that you have a right to personal space—emotional, physical, and spiritual. This is not an act of rebellion against God or the divine, but a way to preserve your mental health and spiritual integrity. Reaffirm your right to have boundaries and make decisions that honor your needs.

Conclusion:

Setting boundaries in spiritual contexts is not only a vital step in healing from spiritual abuse but also a crucial part of reclaiming your personal autonomy and spirituality. Boundaries are not sinful; they are essential for maintaining healthy relationships, both with others and with God. By learning to differentiate between faithfulness and people-pleasing, and by using practical techniques to assert your autonomy, you can create a space where your emotional, physical, and spiritual needs are respected and nurtured. Boundaries empower you to protect your inner world and to cultivate a spirituality that is authentic, resilient, and free from manipulation.

Chapter 8

Reclaiming Your Inner Compass – Trusting Yourself Again

Introduction:

For many who have experienced spiritual abuse, the journey to reclaiming one's inner compass is long and difficult. Spiritual abuse often involves the systematic undermining of personal autonomy, where individuals are taught to distrust their own instincts, judgments, and spiritual experiences. In these environments, external authority—be it a spiritual leader, a community, or institutional doctrine—becomes the ultimate guide, while the individual's inner voice is silenced or dismissed. As a result, many survivors of spiritual abuse are left feeling disconnected from their own intuition, unsure of how to make decisions, and fearful of trusting themselves again.

Reclaiming your inner compass is the process of rediscovering your capacity for self-trust and spiritual discernment. It involves undoing the dependency on external authorities that have shaped your sense of self and reestablishing your connection with your own inner guidance. In this chapter, we will explore how to undo the dependency on external authority, learn the vital skill of discernment over blind obedience, and practice emotional and spiritual self-trust. By the end of this chapter, you will have the tools to reconnect with your authentic self and navigate life with a renewed sense of inner strength and direction.

Undoing Dependency on External "Authority"

For survivors of spiritual abuse, one of the most challenging aspects of reclaiming personal power is untangling the psychological and emotional dependency that has been formed on external authorities. In abusive spiritual environments, external figures—whether they are religious leaders, spiritual guides, or institutional teachings—are elevated to a position of ultimate authority. These figures dictate not only what to believe but also how to think, feel, and behave. This external dependency is reinforced through manipulation, control, and the instilling of fear.

Recognizing the Cycle of Dependency

The first step in undoing this dependency is recognizing how it operates. Dependency on external authority often starts with a genuine desire for guidance, community, or spiritual direction. However, in abusive environments, this natural need is exploited, and the individual's ability to make their own decisions becomes increasingly compromised. The abuser or authority figure may portray themselves as the only true source of spiritual truth, leading followers to believe that their personal connection to the divine is inadequate or invalid.

You may notice that in your past, you were taught to seek the approval or guidance of others before making even the most basic decisions—whether they were personal, emotional, or spiritual. This dependency on external authority can feel all-encompassing, leaving you uncertain of your own path, values, and desires. The fear of making a wrong decision, facing punishment, or displeasing the authority figure can create paralysis and confusion.

Reclaiming Your Authority

To undo this dependency, you must begin by acknowledging that you are your own authority. This does not mean abandoning your faith or rejecting spiritual guidance altogether, but rather learning to distinguish between healthy guidance and manipulation. Reclaiming your authority means recognizing that your thoughts, feelings, and beliefs are valid, and that you have the right to explore, question, and decide for yourself.

A powerful first step in reclaiming your inner authority is to set boundaries with the external influences that have been controlling or manipulative. This may involve distancing yourself from certain communities or individuals who continue to impose their beliefs on you. It might also mean setting emotional, intellectual, and spiritual boundaries by deciding which teachings or practices serve your authentic growth and which ones are simply attempts to control you.

Another important practice in reclaiming your authority is giving yourself permission to make mistakes and learn from them. Recognize that your journey is unique, and it is okay to explore different spiritual practices or belief systems without needing approval from others. Trust that your own path will unfold in its own time and according to your own rhythm.

Learning Discernment Over Blind Obedience

In spiritually abusive contexts, obedience is often framed as a moral or spiritual virtue—especially blind obedience to an authority figure. Disobedience is labeled as rebellion, sin, or spiritual immaturity. As a result, survivors of spiritual abuse may struggle with discerning between obedience that is healthy and necessary, and obedience that is motivated by fear, control, or manipulation. The goal of reclaiming your inner compass is to shift from blind obedience to discernment—learning to evaluate spiritual teachings, practices, and relationships based on your own inner wisdom, rather than external pressure.

The Importance of Discernment

Discernment is the ability to perceive and distinguish truth from falsehood, to trust your intuition, and to make decisions that align with your values and well-being. It is not about rejecting all forms of authority but learning to critically evaluate what is true and beneficial for you. Discernment allows you to make decisions that resonate with your authentic self, free from coercion, manipulation, or guilt.

In the context of spiritual abuse, learning discernment involves evaluating teachings, leaders, and practices in a way that honors your own experience of God, spirituality, and truth. This can be a slow process, especially if you've been conditioned to blindly accept authority. However, with practice, discernment becomes a powerful tool for spiritual self-preservation.

Here are some key principles of discernment to incorporate into your life:

1. **Trust Your Intuition**: Your intuition is a vital source of wisdom and guidance. When something feels off or misaligned with your true self, trust that feeling. Discernment begins with listening to your gut and learning to differentiate between the voice of truth and the voice of manipulation.

2. **Ask Critical Questions**: Don't be afraid to ask questions, even about sacred or deeply held beliefs. Healthy spirituality encourages inquiry and growth, while manipulation thrives on unquestioning obedience. Asking questions is a sign of strength, not rebellion. When faced with a belief or practice that doesn't sit well with you, explore it critically—research it, meditate on it, and seek the counsel of trusted individuals who are aligned with your values.

3. **Align with Your Values**: Discernment involves making decisions that reflect your personal values and spiritual beliefs. As you deconstruct your past experiences and reconnect with your inner compass, you will begin to recognize what feels true to you—whether it's a particular practice, relationship, or teaching. Trust that your personal alignment with these values is just as valid as any external doctrine or guideline.

4. **Observe the Fruits**: In evaluating whether something is truly aligned with your spiritual path, consider the fruits it produces. Does it bring peace, growth, and love into your life? Or does it

lead to confusion, fear, and shame? A healthy spiritual practice and authority should lead to empowerment and liberation, not fear and control.

Emotional and Spiritual Self-Trust Practices

Trusting yourself again after spiritual abuse requires both emotional and spiritual work. This process involves healing the wounds of self-doubt and rebuilding your connection to your inner wisdom. Self-trust is not something that happens overnight—it requires time, patience, and consistent effort. Below are some practices that can help you develop emotional and spiritual self-trust.

1. Journaling and Reflection

Journaling is a powerful practice for reconnecting with your inner self. It allows you to process your thoughts, emotions, and spiritual experiences in a safe, private space. When navigating spiritual abuse or deconstructing your faith, journaling can help you separate your authentic voice from the influences of others.

Try writing down your thoughts and reflections after prayer, meditation, or spiritual practices. Record any doubts, questions, or experiences that arise. Over time, you will begin to notice patterns in your thoughts and feelings, which can help guide your decision-making and discernment.

2. Meditation and Mindfulness

Meditation and mindfulness are essential practices for quieting the mind and reconnecting with your inner wisdom. These practices help you tune into your body, emotions, and spirit, allowing you to cultivate a deep sense of self-awareness. Mindfulness teaches you to be present with your thoughts and feelings without judgment, helping you listen to your intuition more clearly.

Incorporating daily meditation or mindfulness practices into your routine can enhance your ability to trust your own guidance and intuition. It provides a space for inner reflection, allowing you to process the healing journey and gain clarity about your spiritual path.

3. Affirmations and Self-Compassion

Rebuilding self-trust involves developing a compassionate relationship with yourself. Affirmations are a tool that can help rewire negative self-beliefs that may have been instilled by spiritual abuse. Start each day with affirmations that affirm your worth, your autonomy, and your ability to trust yourself. For example, say to yourself: "I trust my intuition," "My feelings are valid," or "I am capable of making choices that align with my truth."

Additionally, practice self-compassion. Recognize that healing takes time and that it's okay to make mistakes along the way. Be gentle with yourself and acknowledge the courage it takes to rebuild your connection to your inner compass.

4. Seek Guidance from Trusted Sources

While the goal is to reclaim your own authority, it's important to surround yourself with supportive, trustworthy individuals who encourage your spiritual growth and personal development. This could include spiritual mentors, counselors, or communities that respect your autonomy and encourage independent thinking. Having a network of people who honor your journey can help reinforce your sense of self-trust.

Conclusion:

Reclaiming your inner compass and trusting yourself again after spiritual abuse is a transformative process that requires patience, courage, and consistent effort. Undoing dependency on external authority, learning discernment over blind obedience, and practicing emotional and spiritual self-trust are vital steps in reclaiming your autonomy and connection to the divine. As you reclaim your power, trust that you have the capacity to navigate your spiritual journey with confidence, authenticity, and wisdom. Your inner compass is not only a guide for making decisions—it is a reflection of your true self, aligned with your deepest values, desires, and connection to the divine. Trust it, nurture it, and allow it to lead you toward a spirituality that is deeply empowering and free from manipulation.

PART III
BEYOND THE PULPIT –
HEALING AND REDEFINING
PEACE

Chapter 9

Healing Isn't Heresy – Therapy, Community, and God

Introduction:

Healing from spiritual abuse is a complex, multifaceted journey that involves not only healing the wounds inflicted by others but also reestablishing a healthy relationship with both your mental health and spirituality. Many survivors of spiritual abuse find themselves at a crossroads, wondering if healing is even possible without sacrificing their faith. This internal struggle often arises because healing is seen by some as a departure from faith, or even as an act of heresy. However, healing is not a betrayal of your spirituality—it is an essential part of reclaiming your relationship with God, yourself, and others.

This chapter will explore how therapy, community, and spirituality can work together in the healing process. We will discuss how to find trauma-informed therapists who understand the unique challenges of faith harm, the role of community in supporting your journey to wholeness, and how mental health and spirituality can coexist in a healthy, balanced way. The ultimate goal is to show that healing is not a betrayal of your faith but a process that leads you toward a more integrated, whole, and empowered life.

Finding Trauma-Informed Therapists Who Understand Faith Harm

When seeking therapy after experiencing spiritual abuse, it's crucial to find a professional who is not only trauma-informed but also understands the specific nature of faith harm. Traditional trauma therapy is essential for healing, but when spiritual abuse is involved, it's important that your therapist is sensitive to the spiritual aspects of your pain. Trauma-informed therapy focuses on understanding how past traumatic events affect mental health and provides strategies for coping with the emotional and psychological effects of trauma.

Why Faith Harm Needs Special Consideration

Spiritual abuse is unique in that it involves deep, often systemic violations of trust, belief, and identity. It can be difficult for survivors to separate their spiritual wounds from emotional or psychological wounds, particularly when their faith and identity were intertwined with the abusive system. A therapist who understands faith harm can help survivors navigate this intersection, acknowledging that both their emotional and spiritual wounds need to be healed simultaneously.

Survivors of spiritual abuse often experience complex trauma, including:

- **Disillusionment with God**: Feeling betrayed by a figure they once trusted deeply.

- **Loss of spiritual identity**: Struggling to reconcile their faith and identity after the damage done by an abusive system.

- **Guilt and shame**: Internalized messages that questioning faith is sinful or rebellious.

- **Fear of spiritual isolation**: The belief that healing means walking away from a relationship with God or being ostracized from the faith community.

A trauma-informed therapist will not only help you heal from the emotional scars left by spiritual abuse but also assist you in reconstructing your spiritual beliefs in a healthy and empowering way. They will respect your beliefs, offer validation, and provide the tools to heal without forcing you to choose between mental health and spirituality.

How to Find a Trauma-Informed Therapist

Finding a therapist who understands both trauma and faith harm can be challenging, but it is possible. Here are a few ways to find the right professional:

1. **Look for Specialized Credentials**: Seek therapists who have experience with trauma or who specialize in religious trauma. Look for certifications in trauma therapy (e.g., Certified Trauma Professional, EMDR) and, if possible, those with experience working with survivors of spiritual or religious abuse.

2. **Research Religious Background or Sensitivity**: Some therapists have experience working with clients from specific religious backgrounds, which can be helpful in understanding the nuances of faith harm. You may want to look for someone who

respects your spiritual path and is willing to discuss religious issues openly and without judgment.

3. **Online Directories and Networks**: Many online directories, such as the *Religious Trauma Institute* or *Psychology Today*, offer filters to help you find therapists who specialize in religious or spiritual trauma. You can search by location, specialty, and even faith background to find the right match.

4. **Ask Questions**: Don't be afraid to ask potential therapists about their experience with religious trauma or their views on spirituality. You might want to ask, "How do you approach clients who have experienced spiritual abuse?" or "What is your experience working with clients who are rebuilding their faith?"

The right therapist can help you process the trauma of spiritual abuse while honoring your faith and helping you rebuild a healthier relationship with both your mental and spiritual life.

The Role of Community in Healing

The importance of community in the healing process cannot be overstated. Spiritual abuse often leads to deep isolation, both from others and from the faith community. Spiritual abusers thrive on creating divisions—between members, between the individual and their family or friends, and even between the individual and God. As a result, many survivors of spiritual abuse feel utterly alone, struggling to rebuild trust in others or in any form of spiritual fellowship.

Finding a Safe and Supportive Community

Healing from spiritual abuse involves reestablishing meaningful, healthy relationships, and finding a supportive community is one of the most important steps in the process. The right community can provide emotional validation, a sense of belonging, and encouragement along the journey of healing.

When seeking out a new community or returning to a community after experiencing spiritual abuse, it's important to consider the following:

1. **A Community That Respects Boundaries**: A supportive community will respect your personal boundaries and give you space to heal at your own pace. They will not pressure you to conform or to engage in practices that make you uncomfortable.

2. **Non-Judgmental Support**: Look for a group that allows room for questioning, vulnerability, and personal growth. You should be able to voice your doubts, struggles, and emotions without fear of condemnation or dismissal.

3. **Spiritual Freedom**: A healthy community should allow you to engage in your spiritual practices freely and authentically, without coercion or manipulation. You should be encouraged to explore your relationship with God in a way that feels safe and empowering.

4. **Peer Support**: Healing from spiritual abuse is easier when you can connect with others who have had similar experiences.

Support groups or online forums for survivors of spiritual abuse can be incredibly helpful, as they provide validation, shared understanding, and the opportunity to learn from others who have walked the same path.

5. **Rebuild Faith and Belonging**: Healing doesn't mean abandoning your faith, and a supportive community will honor that. Look for groups that encourage you to rebuild your relationship with God in a healthy, non-controlling way.

A supportive community is essential for healing because it provides emotional connection and helps reduce the feelings of isolation that spiritual abuse often causes. Through fellowship with others who understand your pain, you can begin to heal in a way that honors both your emotional and spiritual needs.

How Spirituality and Mental Health Can Coexist

One of the most important realizations in healing from spiritual abuse is that mental health and spirituality are not mutually exclusive. In fact, they can work together to create a holistic, integrated approach to healing. While some may view therapy as something that conflicts with spiritual healing, they can actually complement each other beautifully when approached with an open mind and heart.

Integrating Mental Health and Spirituality

Healing from spiritual abuse often involves recognizing that mental health practices—such as therapy, self-care, and emotional regulation—are essential for spiritual well-being. Likewise, spiritual practices—such as prayer, meditation, and mindfulness—can provide profound benefits for mental health. The key is understanding that both realms contribute to your overall healing and that one does not need to be sacrificed for the other.

1. **Healing the Mind and Spirit**: Therapy can help you heal emotional wounds, while spirituality provides a sense of purpose, connection, and transcendence. When these two forces work in tandem, they create a powerful foundation for healing. For example, therapy can help you process trauma, while spiritual practices can help you reconnect with your faith and find peace.

2. **Self-Care as a Spiritual Practice**: Taking care of your mental health through self-care practices—such as rest, exercise, mindfulness, and therapy—is a spiritual practice in itself. It is an act of honoring your body, mind, and soul. Spirituality can be integrated into mental health by recognizing that caring for yourself is a way of honoring the divine, whether you are healing emotionally, physically, or spiritually.

3. **Spiritual Practices to Complement Therapy**: Many survivors find that certain spiritual practices can be incredibly helpful in supporting their mental health. Meditation, prayer, journaling, or spending time in nature can bring clarity, peace, and comfort, aiding in the emotional healing process. These practices can be integrated into the therapeutic process to promote overall well-being.

4. **No Conflict Between Faith and Therapy**: It's essential to understand that seeking therapy doesn't mean abandoning your faith. Therapy can help you clarify and heal from the abuse you've experienced, while spirituality can provide the emotional strength and resilience to continue your journey. The two can coexist without conflict, each supporting the other as you rebuild a life that is whole, balanced, and spiritually fulfilling.

Conclusion:

Healing from spiritual abuse requires the integration of therapy, community, and spirituality. Finding a trauma-informed therapist who understands faith harm, reconnecting with a supportive community, and embracing a holistic approach to healing that incorporates both mental health and spirituality are all crucial elements in the recovery process. By acknowledging that healing is not heresy but a vital part of reclaiming your spiritual and emotional well-being, you can move forward in your journey with greater clarity, resilience, and strength. Your mental health and your spirituality are both sacred, and together they can create a foundation for a life that is not only healed but thriving.

Chapter 10

Family, Fellowship, and Fallout – When You're Still in the Middle of It

Introduction:

Navigating relationships with family, friends, and fellow believers after experiencing spiritual abuse can be one of the most challenging aspects of the healing journey. In many cases, the fallout from spiritual abuse is not limited to the abusive figures or religious communities; it extends to your personal relationships. Those who are still devout or aligned with the abusive system can make the process of healing feel even more complicated. Whether it's facing spiritual shaming, excommunication, or ostracism, the emotional weight of these relationships can leave you feeling stuck between two worlds—one that you are trying to escape and another that still holds tight to beliefs and practices that hurt you.

This chapter will explore how to navigate these difficult relationships—particularly with family members, friends, and religious communities that may still be entrenched in the same abusive structures. We will discuss how to manage the emotional turmoil caused by spiritual shaming, excommunication, or ostracism, and offer practical scripts and strategies to stay grounded when everything around you seems to pull you back into the toxic system. Understanding that healing doesn't mean severing all ties with your past, but rather finding ways to set boundaries and maintain your sense of self, is essential for those still in the middle of the fallout from spiritual abuse.

Navigating Relationships with Still-Devout or Abusive People

After experiencing spiritual abuse, the challenge of navigating relationships with those who are still devout, or who may have been complicit in the abuse, is a source of immense emotional tension. Family members, close friends, or fellow believers may still adhere to the same religious systems, practices, and beliefs that you are now distancing yourself from. These individuals may not understand why you've chosen to leave the community or question its teachings, and their responses can range from concern to outright hostility. This dissonance between your journey and theirs can leave you feeling isolated, misunderstood, or torn between loyalty and self-preservation.

The Emotional Strain of Diverging Paths

One of the most painful aspects of navigating relationships with still-devout or abusive people is the emotional strain it creates. On one hand, you may feel a deep longing for connection, as these relationships—whether with family or close friends—were once a vital part of your life and identity. On the other hand, there may be anger, confusion, and hurt from the abuse you experienced within the same spiritual context. The dissonance between your current beliefs and theirs can create a profound emotional conflict: how can you stay connected to people you love, but who are still aligned with the very system that caused you harm?

This struggle is especially intense when the relationships in question are family-based. Family members are often the people we feel the most loyalty and attachment to, and the emotional difficulty of distancing oneself from them can be overwhelming. It may feel like a betrayal of the familial bond, and the pressure to stay aligned with their beliefs—especially if they still hold those beliefs as sacred—can cause confusion and guilt. However, it's important to recognize that maintaining relationships with family members or friends who are still devout does not mean sacrificing your personal healing or beliefs. Setting boundaries and learning how to communicate effectively with these individuals can create the necessary space for your growth without compromising your emotional and spiritual well-being.

Differentiating Between Genuine Concern and Manipulation

When navigating relationships with still-devout or abusive individuals, it's essential to differentiate between genuine concern for your well-being and manipulative behaviors that seek to maintain control over you. Religious communities that use guilt, shame, or fear to manipulate their members often do so under the guise of concern for your soul or salvation. Family members or friends who are still devout may express their concern in ways that feel controlling, dismissive of your autonomy, or invalidating of your experiences.

It's crucial to recognize when someone is genuinely concerned for you, versus when they are attempting to manipulate you back into the system or beliefs that harmed you. Common manipulative tactics include:

- **Guilt-tripping**: "You're abandoning your faith" or "How can you walk away from God?"

- **Spiritual shaming**: "You'll never be truly happy without God" or "You're making a mistake that will cost you in the end."

- **Threatening consequences**: "If you continue down this path, you'll be separated from us forever" or "God will punish you for rejecting His plan."

Recognizing these tactics allows you to set emotional boundaries and protect your sense of self. You are under no obligation to explain, justify, or defend your journey to anyone—especially if their concern is rooted in the need to control or manipulate you.

Setting Boundaries with Family and Friends

Setting boundaries with family members and friends who are still devout is a crucial part of the healing process. Boundaries allow you to protect yourself from further harm while maintaining relationships in a way that is healthy for you. However, this is not always an easy process, especially when deep emotional ties are involved.

Here are a few strategies to help you set healthy boundaries:

1. **Be Clear About Your Needs**: Clearly communicate your need for space, emotional support, or understanding. For example, you might say, "I need to take a break from discussing religion for a

while," or "I'm not ready to discuss my beliefs with you right now."

2. **Establish Limits on Emotional Conversations**: When conversations begin to veer into guilt, shame, or religious manipulation, calmly but firmly set limits. You could say, "I understand that you have concerns, but I need to focus on my emotional healing right now."

3. **Don't Engage in Spiritual Arguments**: Spiritual debates often turn into emotionally charged arguments. If you feel yourself becoming defensive or upset, it's okay to say, "I'm not ready for this conversation" and walk away.

4. **Be Prepared for Pushback**: Setting boundaries with still-devout individuals may lead to resistance. Prepare yourself emotionally for possible rejection or hostility, and remind yourself that your boundaries are necessary for your healing.

Managing Spiritual Shaming, Excommunication, or Ostracism

The fallout from spiritual abuse may include spiritual shaming, excommunication, or ostracism—whether these consequences are explicit or implied. These actions are often used by abusive religious communities to punish those who question, challenge, or leave the system. They are designed to instill fear, guilt, and shame, and to reinforce the belief that leaving the community means spiritual death or damnation.

Spiritual Shaming: The Silent Weapon

Spiritual shaming occurs when individuals are made to feel unworthy, sinful, or spiritually defective for questioning or leaving their religious community. Survivors of spiritual abuse often encounter shaming from family members, friends, or fellow believers who view their doubts or departure as a personal betrayal. This shaming can be subtle—expressed through disappointment, coldness, or judgmental comments—or more overt, such as accusations of being spiritually immature or rebellious.

To manage spiritual shaming, it is crucial to:

- **Recognize the Source of Shame**: Spiritual shame is often a weapon used by controlling individuals or institutions to maintain power. Remind yourself that this shame is not a reflection of your worth but a reflection of others' need to control you.

- **Reject the Narrative of Unworthiness**: Reclaim your sense of self-worth. Your decision to leave or question a harmful system is a brave and empowered choice. You are worthy of love and respect, regardless of the opinions of others.

- **Find Healing in Self-Compassion**: Counteract the shame with self-compassion. Recognize the strength it takes to walk away from an abusive environment and the courage it takes to honor your own emotional and spiritual needs.

Excommunication and Ostracism: Facing the Fear of Rejection

Excommunication or ostracism are tactics often used by religious communities to isolate and punish those who leave or challenge the group. These actions can feel devastating, especially when they come from people you love and trust. The fear of rejection—whether from family, friends, or your former faith community—can cause intense emotional pain.

However, it is essential to remember that excommunication or ostracism is not a reflection of your worth or spirituality. It is a tool of control that abusive systems use to keep people within their grasp. While the loss of connection may feel painful, it is also an opportunity for you to reclaim your autonomy and build a new, healthier support system.

To manage excommunication or ostracism, consider the following:

1. **Acknowledge the Pain**: The loss of community and the pain of rejection are real and valid. Allow yourself to grieve the relationships and connections that are lost, without internalizing the idea that your worth is diminished because of others' choices.

2. **Seek New Communities of Support**: While the loss of community may feel isolating, it is also an opportunity to build new, healthy relationships. Seek out support groups, online communities, or like-minded individuals who can offer validation, understanding, and connection during this time.

3. **Focus on Personal Healing**: The process of rebuilding your life outside the abusive system requires time and emotional energy. Focus on healing from the trauma you've experienced, cultivating self-compassion, and rebuilding your sense of spiritual and emotional wholeness.

Scripts and Strategies for Staying Grounded

Dealing with the emotional fallout of spiritual abuse, especially when still connected to people in the same religious system, can be overwhelming. Developing scripts and strategies to stay grounded can help you navigate these difficult interactions with more clarity, confidence, and emotional resilience.

Scripts for Handling Manipulative or Guilt-Tripping Conversations

When faced with guilt, shame, or manipulation from those who are still devout or complicit in the abusive system, it can be helpful to have prepared responses that protect your boundaries and preserve your emotional well-being.

1. **Setting Boundaries on Religious Conversations**: "I understand that you care about my spiritual well-being, but I am not ready to discuss my beliefs right now. Please respect that."

2. **Responding to Guilt-Tripping**: "I hear that you're concerned, but I am taking the time I need to heal and figure things out for myself. I'm not making decisions out of spite or rebellion, but out of a desire for personal growth and peace."

3. **Responding to Spiritual Shaming**: "I appreciate that you care about my soul, but I am on my own spiritual journey. This doesn't mean I don't value you or your beliefs, but I need to take time for myself."

Strategies for Staying Grounded

1. **Self-Affirmations**: Remind yourself daily of your worth, your right to question, and your decision to prioritize your well-being. Affirmations like "I am worthy of love and respect," "My questions are valid," and "I trust myself" can reinforce your self-trust.

2. **Emotional Detachment**: Practice emotional detachment when faced with spiritual shaming or manipulation. Recognize that the pain others project onto you is not yours to carry. Use grounding techniques, such as deep breathing or mindfulness, to stay connected to your own sense of self.

3. **Building Emotional Resilience**: Strengthen your emotional resilience by focusing on self-care, setting healthy boundaries, and cultivating a support system that honors your healing. Over time, your ability to stay grounded in your truth will grow stronger, even in the face of external pressure.

Conclusion:

Navigating relationships with still-devout or abusive individuals after spiritual abuse is one of the most challenging aspects of the healing process. The emotional pain of facing spiritual shaming, excommunication, or ostracism can be overwhelming, but it's important to remember that healing is not about appeasing others or staying within the system that caused you harm. It's about reclaiming your autonomy, protecting your emotional and spiritual well-being, and building relationships that honor your authentic self. By setting healthy boundaries, differentiating between genuine concern and manipulation, and using grounding strategies, you can move through this difficult phase with confidence, self-compassion, and strength. Healing is possible, and it begins with trusting yourself and your journey.

Chapter 11

Rebuilding Faith (Or Not) – What Comes After Deconstruction

Introduction:

Deconstruction is not an end, but rather a beginning. For many who have experienced spiritual abuse, the process of deconstructing faith is not about rejecting spirituality entirely but about rebuilding it on a foundation that is more authentic, empowering, and freeing. Yet, for some, deconstruction leaves them with more questions than answers. As the walls of their former beliefs come down, they are left standing at the crossroads, unsure of what to build next. In the aftermath of spiritual deconstruction, the question arises: what comes after the unraveling? Can faith be rebuilt, or is it time to explore new paths, whether that means embracing agnosticism, mysticism, or an entirely different tradition?

This chapter will explore how to navigate the uncertain and often daunting journey of rebuilding faith (or choosing not to) after deconstruction. It will discuss the importance of choosing your own beliefs with integrity, finding sacredness in unexpected places, and embracing faith without fear—whether that means reconstructing your old faith with new understanding, exploring alternative spiritual paths, or embracing uncertainty. By the end of this chapter, you will have the tools and frameworks to continue your spiritual journey with authenticity and confidence, embracing your newfound freedom while respecting your unique journey.

Choosing Your Own Beliefs with Integrity

One of the most powerful outcomes of spiritual deconstruction is the opportunity to choose your own beliefs with integrity. Many individuals who experience spiritual abuse find that their beliefs were shaped by external pressures, fear, and manipulation rather than personal conviction or authentic spiritual experiences. Deconstruction is a process of questioning those external influences and discovering what resonates with you on a deep, personal level. But as the foundation crumbles, how do you rebuild?

The Challenge of Freedom

The challenge after deconstruction is that, for the first time, you may feel completely free to believe—or not believe—anything you choose. This newfound freedom can be both exhilarating and overwhelming. No longer bound by the rigid doctrines or practices of a particular religious system, you are free to explore spirituality on your own terms. Yet, this freedom also requires you to take responsibility for your beliefs and the way they shape your life.

Choosing your beliefs with integrity means aligning your spiritual journey with your values, experiences, and inner truths. It requires you to reflect on the core of what matters most to you and what feels most aligned with your authentic self. For some, this may mean returning to their faith with new insights, while for others, it may mean charting an entirely new course. The key is to choose beliefs that resonate deeply with your sense of truth and integrity, rather than beliefs that serve external expectations or provide comfort in the absence of clarity.

Authentic Spirituality: Trusting Yourself

An important aspect of choosing your beliefs with integrity is trusting yourself. For many survivors of spiritual abuse, the trauma of manipulation and control has eroded self-trust. You may have been taught to question your own spiritual experiences or ignore your inner wisdom in favor of external authority. Rebuilding your beliefs means learning to trust your inner guidance again.

To rebuild faith with integrity, begin by asking yourself:

1. **What resonates with me?** Reflect on what beliefs, practices, or spiritual experiences have felt true and meaningful to you, even before deconstruction. Trust the wisdom in your heart, and consider what you believe in spite of the external forces that have shaped your faith in the past.

2. **What do I value spiritually?** Think about what principles or values are non-negotiable for you. Whether it's love, compassion, justice, freedom, or connection to the divine, make these values the foundation of your new beliefs.

3. **What can I let go of?** Deconstructing your faith involves releasing old beliefs, practices, or teachings that no longer serve you. This may include beliefs that were used to control you,

manipulate you, or shame you. Letting go of these is not a rejection of spirituality but a reclaiming of your own power to choose what is life-giving and authentic.

Embracing Evolution

As you rebuild your beliefs, recognize that your faith may continue to evolve. What you believe today may not be the same as what you believe tomorrow, and that's okay. True spiritual growth involves change, questioning, and discovery. Allow yourself to be open to new insights, experiences, and understandings without clinging to one fixed set of beliefs. Spirituality is not a destination but a journey, and your beliefs may transform as you continue to explore and grow.

Finding Sacredness in Unexpected Places

After deconstructing a rigid, institutionalized faith, you may find that sacredness can be found in unexpected places—away from the walls of a church, the pages of a holy book, or the rituals of a prescribed tradition. Many survivors of spiritual abuse experience a deep sense of disillusionment with the systems that once defined their spirituality. In this disillusionment, however, lies an opportunity to reconnect with the sacred in more expansive, inclusive, and personal ways.

Sacredness Beyond Religious Institutions

Sacredness does not have to be tied to a religious institution or a prescribed set of practices. It can be found in nature, in the quiet moments of solitude, in the connection between people, or in the deep sense of awe and wonder at the world around us. For those who have experienced spiritual harm, reconnecting with the sacred outside of traditional religious contexts can be a powerful way to heal.

Examples of finding sacredness in unexpected places may include:

- **Nature**: Many people find a deep sense of connection to the divine when in nature. Whether walking through a forest, standing on a mountain, or simply sitting by a stream, nature has a way of evoking a sense of awe and reverence that transcends institutionalized religion.

- **Art and Creativity**: For some, sacredness is found in the act of creating—whether through painting, writing, music, or other forms of artistic expression. Creativity can be a way of connecting with the divine by channeling personal expression and emotional healing through art.

- **Community**: Sacredness can also be found in authentic, loving, and supportive communities. These communities do not have to be religious in nature but are grounded in principles of mutual respect, love, and shared humanity.

- **Acts of Service**: For some, sacredness is found in helping others, in compassion, and in acts of kindness. These moments of service can be deeply spiritual and transformative.

Reimagining Spirituality: Embracing Mysticism and the Unknown

After deconstructing your faith, you may find that embracing mystery and the unknown is a vital part of the healing process. Mysticism—the exploration of direct, personal experiences of the divine—offers an alternative to rigid religious dogma. Mystical spirituality emphasizes personal experience, intuition, and connection with the divine outside of traditional structures.

Embracing mysticism involves:

- **Being Open to Uncertainty**: Mysticism requires embracing uncertainty and allowing yourself to experience the divine in ways that are not confined to dogma or rigid belief systems. It is a form of spirituality that encourages exploration, openness, and flexibility.

- **Intuitive Spirituality**: Mysticism encourages trusting your inner sense of spiritual truth. It recognizes that the divine can be encountered in moments of deep intuition, stillness, or awe, rather than through external authorities or written doctrines.

- **Experiential Connection**: Instead of relying solely on texts or rituals, mysticism values personal experience as a valid and powerful way to connect with the divine. This could include meditation, prayer, altered states of consciousness, or profound moments of insight.

Faith Without Fear: Embracing Agnosticism, Mysticism, or a New Tradition

For some, deconstruction leads to the realization that traditional faith systems no longer resonate with their inner truth. The concept of "faith without fear" is a faith that is free from coercion, manipulation, or control. It is a spirituality that does not demand blind obedience or conformity to rigid doctrines. Embracing faith without fear allows for the possibility of agnosticism, mysticism, or embracing a new spiritual tradition that feels more authentic and aligned with your values.

Agnosticism: Embracing the Unknown

Agnosticism is not a rejection of the divine or spirituality but an honest acknowledgment of the limitations of human understanding. It is the recognition that there is much about existence, the divine, and the universe that remains unknown and perhaps unknowable. For some, agnosticism provides a place of peace—allowing them to let go of the need for certainty and embrace the mystery of life.

Agnostic spirituality is rooted in:

- **Openness to Possibility**: Rather than claiming to have all the answers, agnosticism allows you to live with open-ended questions, seeking truth without the pressure to definitively define it.

- **Embracing Humility**: Agnosticism invites a sense of humility, recognizing that human knowledge and perception are limited. It frees you from the burden of having to be certain about every spiritual or existential question.

- **Living in the Mystery**: Agnosticism embraces the unknown as a source of spiritual exploration. It allows you to experience awe, wonder, and mystery without needing to claim definitive answers or explanations.

Embracing Mysticism or a New Tradition

For others, deconstruction opens the door to embracing mysticism or exploring new spiritual traditions. Mysticism and alternative spiritual paths do not have to reject the divine but allow for a broader, more inclusive approach to spirituality. These paths often emphasize direct experiences of the divine, personal intuition, and a sense of oneness with the universe.

Embracing a new tradition might involve exploring:

- **Spirituality Outside of Religion**: Exploring practices such as mindfulness, meditation, or yoga can provide a spiritual connection that is not tied to any specific religious system. These practices often focus on inner peace, self-awareness, and connection to the greater whole.

- **Reconstructing Faith with a New Lens**: For some, deconstruction leads to a rebuilding of their faith with a new understanding. This might involve returning to core spiritual values, such as love, compassion, and justice, without being bound by institutionalized beliefs or practices.

- **Mystical and Indigenous Traditions**: Some survivors of spiritual abuse are drawn to mystical or indigenous spiritual practices, which often emphasize personal experience, interconnectedness with nature, and the honoring of the divine in all aspects of life.

Conclusion:

The journey after deconstruction is not one-size-fits-all. Some will rebuild their faith in a way that is authentic and empowering, while others may choose a different path altogether—whether that means embracing agnosticism, mysticism, or an entirely new tradition. What matters most is that you are choosing your spiritual path with integrity, based on your personal values, experiences, and inner truth.

Faith without fear is about reclaiming your spiritual autonomy and finding a connection to the divine that is free from manipulation, fear, and shame. It is about trusting yourself and your journey, even if that means venturing into the unknown. Whether you rebuild your faith, embrace a new tradition, or walk a path of spiritual curiosity and openness, know that this journey is yours to navigate. You are free to explore, question, and grow in your spirituality, and in doing so, you reclaim your power and your peace.

Chapter 12

Becoming the Voice You Needed – Advocacy, Art, and Impact

Introduction:

After experiencing spiritual abuse, many survivors find themselves grappling not only with emotional and psychological wounds but also with a profound sense of purpose. For some, the aftermath of abuse can feel overwhelming, like an endless cycle of pain with no clear path forward. However, what often emerges from this suffering is a deep desire to help others, to make a difference, and to turn the pain into something that brings healing—not only for oneself but for others who are still suffering in silence. Advocacy, art, and impact can serve as powerful tools for survivors to channel their experiences into something meaningful, transformative, and healing.

In this chapter, we will explore how survivors of spiritual abuse can turn their pain into purpose through advocacy and creative outlets. By becoming the voice they needed during their struggles, survivors can break the silence, create awareness, and help others who are on the same path to healing. We will also discuss the importance of supporting others while continuing your own journey of recovery, emphasizing that healing doesn't mean sacrificing your well-being to help others—it means finding ways to give back that honor your own needs and boundaries.

Turning Pain into Purpose

One of the most empowering aspects of recovery from spiritual abuse is the ability to transform pain into purpose. The emotional, psychological, and spiritual wounds left by abuse often leave survivors with a deep sense of injustice, anger, and sadness. However, many survivors find that the most healing path is not one of retreat or isolation but one of action. Turning your pain into purpose is a way to reclaim control over your narrative, to rise from the ashes of abuse and create something that offers hope and support to others.

Finding Purpose in Pain

For many survivors, the process of turning pain into purpose starts with acknowledging the deep emotional and spiritual scars that have been left behind. It's essential to give yourself permission to grieve the loss of your former spiritual life and the relationships that were damaged or severed as a result of abuse. Grieving this loss is not a sign of weakness, but rather a critical part of the healing process.

Once you've allowed yourself to process the pain, the next step is to explore how that pain can be channeled into something meaningful. This process involves reflecting on your experiences, your values, and your desires for the future. What motivates you to keep going despite everything you've endured? What are the core beliefs and values that have sustained you through the toughest parts of your journey?

The pain you've experienced can become a wellspring of wisdom and strength. As a survivor of spiritual abuse, you are uniquely positioned to understand the struggles of others who have faced similar experiences. Your story, your voice, and your healing process can offer light to those still in the darkness, showing them that recovery is possible and that they are not alone.

Reclaiming Your Voice

For many survivors of spiritual abuse, one of the most profound aspects of their healing journey is reclaiming their voice. Spiritual abuse often involves silencing the individual, stripping them of their autonomy and sense of self. Survivors are taught to prioritize the needs of the group, the church, or the leader over their own voice, desires, and experiences.

Reclaiming your voice means recognizing that your experiences are valid and worthy of being shared. It means refusing to remain silent in the face of injustice and finding the courage to speak your truth. Your voice can be a powerful tool for advocacy, healing, and change.

By sharing your story, you not only begin to heal from your own trauma, but you also give others the permission to do the same. Your voice can help break the cycle of silence and shame, allowing others to feel less isolated and more empowered in their own recovery.

Creative and Advocacy Outlets for Survivors

Creative expression and advocacy work are two powerful avenues for survivors to channel their pain and purpose into something meaningful. Whether through writing, art, public speaking, or activism, these outlets offer a way to transform personal experiences of suffering into societal change and healing.

Art: The Healing Power of Creative Expression

Art has long been recognized as a powerful form of healing. Whether through visual art, music, dance, or writing, creative expression allows survivors of spiritual abuse to process their emotions, understand their experiences, and communicate their feelings in ways that words alone may not be able to capture. Art allows for an outlet that bypasses intellectualization, speaking directly to the heart, and often uncovers aspects of healing that might remain hidden without this form of expression.

1. **Visual Art**: Painting, drawing, photography, or other visual art forms can be a cathartic release for survivors. These mediums allow for a raw and personal exploration of one's journey, and the resulting work can be shared with others or kept as a private reflection of the healing process.

2. **Music and Songwriting**: For some survivors, music offers a deeply personal way to express emotions and connect with others. Writing songs, composing music, or simply singing can be an act of emotional release, a way to communicate pain, hope, or healing in ways that transcend language.

3. **Writing and Poetry**: Writing—whether through personal journals, blogs, or poetry—can help survivors make sense of their experiences. Written words can be a way to claim your story, establish your identity outside of the abusive system, and share your journey with others in a way that resonates deeply.

Advocacy: Raising Awareness and Supporting Change

Advocacy is another vital outlet for survivors. Many survivors find that they can transform their trauma into a force for societal change by raising awareness about spiritual abuse, educating others about the harm that can be caused by toxic religious environments, and working to prevent abuse in the future. Advocacy can take many forms:

1. **Public Speaking**: Sharing your story with larger audiences, whether in person or through digital platforms, can help break the silence surrounding spiritual abuse. Public speaking is an empowering way to advocate for change, raise awareness, and empower others to speak out.

2. **Blogging or Writing Articles**: Many survivors turn to blogging or writing articles to educate others about the realities of spiritual abuse. Writing online allows survivors to reach a broad audience, provide resources, and create safe spaces for others to engage in dialogue.

3. **Supporting Survivors**: As a survivor, you can advocate for others who are still trapped in abusive environments. This can involve mentoring, offering emotional support, or connecting others with resources, counseling, and advocacy groups.

4. **Campaigning for Institutional Reform**: Survivors who feel empowered by their healing may work to change the systems that perpetuate spiritual abuse. This could involve working with organizations that focus on spiritual abuse, challenging abusive

religious systems, or advocating for policies that protect vulnerable individuals from spiritual manipulation.

Healing Through Advocacy

Advocacy and creative outlets for survivors are not only about supporting others; they are also about continuing your own healing. The process of advocating for change, whether through sharing your story or working to raise awareness, is a powerful form of self-empowerment. It allows survivors to reclaim their voices and take control of the narrative that was once stolen from them.

By engaging in advocacy or creative projects, you are not only helping others but also reinforcing your own healing. The act of giving back, of helping others, can create a sense of purpose and meaning that accelerates your own recovery process. However, it's important to recognize that advocacy work can be emotionally taxing, so it is crucial to maintain a balance between supporting others and honoring your own need for rest and healing.

Supporting Others While Continuing Your Own Journey

Helping others in their healing journey is a powerful way to stay connected to your purpose and create a sense of community and support. However, it's vital to recognize that your journey of healing is ongoing, and supporting others should never come at the expense of your own well-being. As a survivor, you are entitled to take breaks, set boundaries, and prioritize your own healing while offering support to others.

Setting Boundaries in Advocacy Work

When engaging in advocacy or helping others who are still recovering, it's important to establish clear boundaries. The emotional toll of supporting others can be heavy, and you may find yourself feeling drained if you are constantly giving of yourself. It's essential to know when to step back, take care of your own needs, and avoid burnout. Setting boundaries allows you to offer your support while maintaining your own emotional health.

1. **Know Your Limits**: It's okay to say no to certain requests for support if you're not emotionally ready. Don't feel guilty for prioritizing your own healing.

2. **Delegate and Share the Load**: Advocacy is not a solo endeavor. Connect with other survivors or allies who are also passionate about raising awareness. Sharing the load ensures that you don't feel overwhelmed or overburdened.

3. **Practice Self-Care**: Supporting others can be fulfilling, but it can also be draining. Make time for self-care practices that nourish your mind, body, and spirit. Exercise, meditation, rest, and creative expression are all important for maintaining balance.

Healing Through Mutual Support

Remember that you do not have to do everything alone. The process of supporting others while continuing your own journey of healing is most effective when done within a network of mutual support. Joining survivor groups, online communities, or attending therapy with others who share similar experiences can provide validation, camaraderie, and encouragement.

By connecting with others who have gone through similar experiences, you create a space where healing can occur collectively. Mutual support not only helps others but also reinforces your own sense of community and shared understanding. As you help others heal, you too will continue to grow, learn, and evolve in your own recovery.

Conclusion:

Becoming the voice you needed after experiencing spiritual abuse is one of the most transformative and empowering acts of healing. Advocacy and creative expression are powerful ways to channel your pain into purpose, turning your experiences into something that not only helps others but also continues to fuel your own journey of recovery. Whether through writing, art, public speaking, or supporting others, you can create an impact that resonates far beyond your own healing process.

At the same time, it's crucial to honor your own needs and continue prioritizing your healing. Supporting others while maintaining your well-being requires balance, self-compassion, and setting healthy boundaries. Your healing is a continual process, and it's important to ensure that your advocacy work is a tool for empowerment, not depletion.

In the end, by becoming the voice you needed, you not only help others but also give yourself permission to fully heal, reclaim your power, and move forward with purpose. Through your voice, your art, and your advocacy, you are making a profound impact—both on others and on yourself.

Chapter 13

Holy Liberation – Peace That No Preacher Can Take Away

Introduction

The experience of spiritual abuse can leave you broken, disconnected, and spiritually adrift. Often, it results in a deep emotional and spiritual scar that is hard to heal, especially when your entire worldview has been shaped by an authoritarian belief system that demanded blind obedience and conformity. The very foundation of who you are—the peace, truth, and identity that once defined you—was hijacked and manipulated in ways that can be difficult to fully grasp.

However, recovery from spiritual abuse offers a new horizon, one of holy liberation—a peace that no preacher, no doctrine, and no external authority can ever take away. Holy liberation is the freedom that arises when you reclaim your inner peace, reassert your own truth, and rediscover your authentic identity. It's the kind of freedom that emerges not from the external validation or approval of others but from your own intrinsic worth and connection to your deeper self.

In this chapter, we will explore how to reclaim peace, truth, and identity after spiritual abuse, how to live spiritually free without the constant pressure to perform or meet external standards, and how to embrace a sense of spiritual liberation that comes from within. This journey is about redefining your relationship with the divine, not based on fear or shame but on love, authenticity, and self-empowerment. And finally, we will offer you encouragement and the reminder that, no matter where you are on this journey, you are not alone, and your soul is still sacred.

Reclaiming Peace, Truth, and Identity

Reclaiming peace, truth, and identity is the foundation of the holy liberation you seek. These essential aspects of who you are have likely been distorted or completely stripped away during your experience with spiritual abuse. The peace that once came from your faith was replaced with anxiety, fear, and confusion. The truth that you held dear was manipulated to control you, and your identity was bound by rules, regulations, and an imposed sense of self-worth that was anything but authentic. To experience holy liberation, you must begin by reclaiming these pillars of your being.

Reclaiming Peace

Peace is often the first thing to be eroded in environments where spiritual abuse takes place. Spiritual abuse is built on manipulation, fear, and control. Instead of being a source of comfort and spiritual growth, your faith became a tool for undermining your sense of safety, autonomy, and peace. Peace was something conditioned by external compliance: "If you do this, you'll have peace," or "If you don't follow the rules, you'll lose peace."

True peace, however, is not conditional. It is not earned through behavior or obedience, nor does it depend on pleasing an external authority. Real peace comes from an internal sense of alignment with who you are and your connection to the divine, whatever form that may take. Reclaiming your peace means freeing yourself from the shackles of fear, guilt, and manipulation.

The process of reclaiming peace starts with recognizing that peace is an internal state. It comes from:

1. **Releasing the Need to Perform**: Spiritual abuse thrives on the idea that your worth is determined by how well you perform, how closely you conform, and how much you serve. Reclaiming peace requires that you let go of this constant need to perform and simply accept yourself as you are—worthy and whole.

2. **Reconnecting with Inner Stillness**: The noise of religious demands, judgment, and fear can drown out your inner voice. Practices such as meditation, prayer, or mindfulness can help you reconnect with a deeper sense of stillness, where you can find peace apart from external expectations.

3. **Letting Go of Fear**: Fear is one of the primary tools used in spiritual abuse. It's the fear of punishment, condemnation, or exclusion. To reclaim peace, you must let go of that fear—of judgment from others, of retribution from God, and of the fear that your decisions will be met with rejection.

4. **Embracing Self-Compassion**: Peace also comes from being kind to yourself. After experiencing spiritual abuse, you may feel

deep shame, guilt, or self-blame. Healing requires that you forgive yourself for the times you couldn't stand up for yourself, for the years spent in an abusive system. True peace is found in self-compassion, where you accept your imperfections and honor your healing journey.

Reclaiming peace is not about returning to an idealized past but finding an inner calm that transcends the chaos that spiritual abuse may have caused in your life. It's about reconnecting to a sense of peace that is yours by right, irrespective of external judgments or abuses.

Reclaiming Truth

Truth is another pillar that is often distorted or erased in spiritually abusive systems. Spiritual abusers work hard to manipulate reality, presenting their version of truth as the only valid one. Over time, the survivor's ability to trust their own experiences and perceptions is damaged, often leading to confusion, self-doubt, and a fear of questioning.

Reclaiming truth is about returning to your own internal compass. It's about trusting your experiences, feelings, and thoughts as valid, independent of the indoctrination you endured. It means rejecting the imposed version of truth that was used to control and manipulate you, and instead seeking your own understanding of what is true.

To reclaim your truth, start by:

1. **Questioning Everything**: After spiritual abuse, you may feel overwhelmed by the need to question everything. You may

wonder whether the faith you grew up with was truly spiritual or simply a tool of control. Start with small steps—questioning the beliefs that once held power over you, the ones that told you what was right, what was wrong, and what you should or shouldn't believe. Don't be afraid to explore, doubt, and challenge.

2. **Validating Your Experience**: Your lived experience is valid, even if it contradicts what you were taught. Spiritual abuse can lead you to question your own feelings and experiences, but your truth is yours to claim. Allow yourself to acknowledge your experiences without judgment or shame.

3. **Trusting Your Intuition**: Your intuition is a sacred guide that can lead you toward your authentic truth. Over time, you may have been taught to distrust your instincts, but as you heal, you can begin to reconnect with your inner wisdom. Your intuition will help guide you as you navigate what feels true for you and what no longer resonates.

4. **Exploring New Perspectives**: Reclaiming truth involves allowing yourself to explore different ideas, philosophies, and spiritual practices. This exploration is not about finding a new belief system but about discovering what aligns with your true self. Your truth may change, and that's okay. Trust the process of evolution.

Reclaiming truth means honoring your own inner knowing and freeing yourself from the constraints of imposed doctrines and beliefs.

It's a journey toward intellectual and spiritual freedom where you learn to trust your own understanding of reality.

Reclaiming Identity

Spiritual abuse often results in a complete loss of identity. Your sense of self was shaped by external pressures and the need to conform, often leading you to forget who you truly are. When you are taught that your identity is tied to compliance with religious norms and beliefs, you lose sight of your inherent worth and individuality.

Reclaiming your identity means rediscovering who you are beyond the labels, expectations, and teachings that have been imposed on you. It's about reconnecting with your authentic self—your passions, your dreams, your desires, and your individuality.

To reclaim your identity, consider:

1. **Rediscovering Your Passions**: What did you love before spiritual abuse began to overshadow your life? Reconnect with the things that brought you joy and fulfillment. These parts of you were never lost; they were just buried beneath the weight of expectations.

2. **Redefining Your Spirituality**: Your spirituality is a personal and sacred journey. Whether you choose to reconnect with your old faith or explore a new path, allow your spirituality to be defined by your own truth and experience, not by external pressures. Your relationship with the divine is yours to shape.

3. **Letting Go of Shame**: Shame is a powerful weapon in spiritual abuse. It convinces you that you are flawed, unworthy, or broken. Reclaiming your identity means releasing the shame that was imposed upon you. You are not defined by the shame of others; you are sacred, whole, and worthy.

4. **Affirming Your Worth**: Daily affirmations of self-worth are an essential part of reclaiming your identity. Remind yourself that you are enough as you are—your worth is inherent, not dependent on the approval of others or the performance in any religious system. Your identity is sacred, and it cannot be taken away.

Reclaiming your identity is about letting go of the false self-created by spiritual abuse and rediscovering the authentic person you are. It's about shedding the layers of shame and expectation and stepping into the fullness of your true self.

Living Spiritually Free Without Performance

One of the most profound aspects of holy liberation is the ability to live spiritually free without the constant pressure to perform. Spiritual abuse thrives on creating environments where individuals are made to feel that their worth is contingent upon their performance, their ability to conform, or their adherence to a set of religious rules. This performance-based spirituality is exhausting and often leads to burnout, anxiety, and a deep sense of spiritual emptiness.

Living spiritually free means rejecting the need to perform in order to be loved or accepted. It means embracing spirituality that is authentic, rooted in personal connection, and free from external validation. In spiritual freedom, there is no need to prove anything to anyone. You are enough, just as you are.

Embracing a Spirituality of Presence

Living spiritually free requires a shift from focusing on "doing" to focusing on "being." Spirituality is not about what you achieve or accomplish, but about your presence in each moment. It is about being fully present in your life, in your relationships, and in your connection to the divine.

1. **Living Mindfully**: Embrace the practice of mindfulness, where you are fully present in the moment. Mindfulness allows you to appreciate the sacredness of ordinary life—whether in nature, in quiet moments of reflection, or in the company of loved ones.

2. **Cultivating Gratitude**: True spirituality is rooted in gratitude for what is, not in striving for what you think you should be. Practice gratitude for the small, everyday moments that are sacred and meaningful, and release the pressure to achieve or prove your worth.

3. **Being Enough**: Understand that you do not need to do anything to prove your worth. You are enough as you are. The love and acceptance you seek from the divine or from others is already present within you. Your worth is intrinsic.

Spiritual Freedom Without Guilt

Spiritual freedom also means letting go of guilt. Many survivors of spiritual abuse carry guilt for questioning beliefs, leaving communities, or stepping away from rigid religious systems. But true spiritual freedom comes when you release the guilt that was imposed upon you and embrace a spirituality that is based on love, authenticity, and self-compassion.

1. **Forgive Yourself**: If you feel guilty for your journey, practice self-forgiveness. You are not responsible for the harm done to you, and you have the right to move forward free from guilt.

2. **Embrace Uncertainty**: Spiritual freedom means embracing the unknown and letting go of the need for certainty. You do not need to have all the answers, and that's okay. Your spiritual journey is yours to navigate, and it is valid even without a clear map.

Final Encouragement: You Are Not Alone, and Your Soul Is Still Sacred

The path to recovery from spiritual abuse can be long and difficult, but know that you are not alone. There is a vast, supportive community of people who have walked this path, and there is a wealth of resources, wisdom, and encouragement available to you.

Your soul is still sacred, regardless of the abuse you've experienced. No matter the trauma you've endured, no matter how far you've wandered from the teachings that once defined you, your connection to the divine remains unbroken. You are worthy of love, peace, and spiritual fulfillment. Your soul is inherently sacred, and it cannot be diminished by the actions of others.

Healing is not a destination, and it is not linear. There will be setbacks, doubts, and moments of pain. But each step forward is a step toward rediscovering your inner peace, your truth, and your authentic identity. You are not defined by the abuse you've experienced; you are defined by the strength, resilience, and beauty that reside within you.

Embrace your holy liberation. It is your birthright. You are free to walk your spiritual journey with authenticity, peace, and the full recognition of your sacredness. No preacher, no doctrine, and no external authority can take that away from you. Your journey is yours to create, and your soul is a divine expression of love and truth.

Epilogue

*H*oly Manipulation: Freedom from Spiritual Abuse and Religious Narcissism is not just a book; it is a call to action, a guide, and a beacon of hope for those who have suffered under the heavy hand of spiritual manipulation and narcissistic control. Throughout this journey, we have explored the depths of spiritual abuse, understood the mechanics of narcissism masquerading as faith, and uncovered the tactics used to manipulate, control, and exploit the very essence of an individual's spiritual journey. More importantly, this book offers survivors the tools to break free from this toxic cycle, reclaim their voice, and rebuild a life of peace, authenticity, and spiritual freedom.

In the chapters that preceded this conclusion, we've touched on the foundational aspects of what it means to recognize spiritual abuse, how to understand its impacts, and how to start the long process of healing. We've looked at the importance of telling your story, understanding your beliefs, and trusting yourself again. These elements form the bedrock upon which survivors can build lives rooted in autonomy, resilience, and inner peace. In doing so, they free themselves from the control of those who have sought to define them, to manipulate them, and to distort their connection to the divine.

The final chapters of this book encourage survivors to take back what was once stolen from them: their peace, their truth, and their identity.

Reclaiming peace is about breaking free from the fear, guilt, and shame that spiritual abuse imposed. Reclaiming truth is about trusting your own wisdom and stepping away from the false doctrines that were once presented as absolute. Reclaiming identity is about rediscovering who you truly are, beyond the confines of a harmful belief system.

At the core of this healing process is the ability to live spiritually free—free from the pressure to perform, free from the need to prove one's worthiness, and free from the toxic cycles of obedience and conformity. True spiritual liberation is not about escaping faith or spirituality; it is about transforming your relationship with the divine into something that is uniquely your own—authentic, empowering, and deeply personal.

The final encouragement is simple yet profound: You are not alone. Your journey is part of a larger community of individuals who are rediscovering their sense of self, reclaiming their power, and forging new paths of spiritual freedom. Your soul is sacred, and it always has been. No preacher, no doctrine, no system of control can take away the essence of who you are or your connection to the divine.

As you continue to heal, to grow, and to reclaim your voice, remember that peace is yours to embrace. The road may be long, but the destination is worth it. This is the beginning of a new chapter in your life, one where you are empowered, where your spiritual journey is defined by your own truth, and where you are free to live as the authentic, whole person you were always meant to be.